WHAT I WISH MY YOUTH LEADER KNEW ABOUT YOUTH MINISTRY

Mike Nappa combines wit, insight, and real-world experience with research from kids to create a practical, engaging guide to the nuts and bolts of youth ministry. Best of all, Mike doesn't just rely on his own experience but asks the experts: teenagers. Their insights will both challenge and affirm. Every youth worker—both veteran and newcomer—will learn something new. The best lesson may be to ask your own kids these kinds of questions!
—**Eugene Roehlkepartain,** director of publishing, Search Institute

This book has caused me to think more clearly, draw closer to students, and put more trust in God to help me figure out today's teenager and strengthen our youth ministry. I really appreciate Mike's balance between helping us see what students want and identifying what they need. Thanks for your help, Mike!
—**Doug Fields,** youth pastor, Saddleback Church, author of *Purpose-Driven Youth Ministry*

When I received a copy of Mike's manuscript, I thought, "Oh no! Not another book on youth ministry." But within minutes I was captivated. Mike's approach in this book is to let teenagers speak for themselves. Sure, he does a great job of introducing his own perspective and he has appropriately read the recommended reading list. But I felt as if teenagers were speaking directly to me. Based on their responses, Mike has given every youth minister dozens of practical ideas, tools, and strategies for developing a youth ministry that truly has an impact. This is an important contribution to the future of the church in America.
—**Kevin Graham Ford,** author of *Jesus for a New Generation*

Mike Nappa's book is cutting-edge because it brings the real and fresh insights from those who are most cutting-edge: teenagers. Their feedback, plus Mike's additional research, makes this publication a must read. Mike adds his own humor, genuineness, experience and passion for teenagers. This book is about how to deliver the message in ways our teenagers can hear and act on. It is a revealing book that brings with it a message of hope about our future generations. God will use this work in a powerful way.
—**Ellen Oldacre,** editor-in-chief, *Living with Teenagers*

Mike Nappa has found a way to get at the very practical heart of youth ministry from the perspective of those to whom it matters most . . . young people. Mike's work is insightful, helpful and probably a bit disconcerting to many who practice youth ministry but don't really know how their students think and feel about what they routinely do. This book should be read by every professional and volunteer youth worker with a vision to reach students for Christ.
—**Ken Garland,** associate professor of Christian education, Talbot School of Theology

Three facts about Mike Nappa make this book a winner. One: He loves teenagers. Two: He respects teenagers. Three: He is a wise and discerning person who seeks answers to important questions. And he knows where to go for the answers. *What I Wish My Youth Leader Knew About Youth Ministry* has lots of hands-on insights. If you care about the next generation, read this book.
—**Dr. Norm Wakefield,** professor of pastoral ministry, Phoenix Seminary

This book takes a little of the guesswork out of sculpting an effective ministry to kids who straddle the GenX and Millennial generations. When it's not surprising us with some of kids' ministry preferences, it's reminding us of the basics we should never forget.
—**Rick Lawrence,** editor, *Group* magazine

What I Wish My Youth Leader Knew About Youth Ministry is exactly the kind of how-to resource that will allow those who lead student ministries to sail smoothly. This book may be the best staff-development investment you'll make this year.

—**Ed Rowell,** editor, *Proclaim, Let's Worship,* and *Growing Churches* magazines

What an eye-opener! Through his surveys and keen insight into the hearts and minds of young people, Mike has presented us with a wealth of new information on youth ministry today—and provided a host of immensely practical ideas on how we can implement changes right now to reach out to kids more effectively. I believe this book will quickly become an essential tool for youth ministers everywhere as we step into the new millennium. I know this is one resource I'll definitely keep within arm's reach.

—**Michael Warden,** youth culture expert and author

What I Wish My Youth Leader Knew About Youth Ministry will help you avoid many mistakes made by those who have gone before you. The information that Mike gathered from the 400 students interviewed is extremely valuable. The answers from these students raise important questions about some of the antiquated methods that are presently being used in reaching and keeping today's teens. This will be a valuable addition to any youth worker's library.

—**Les Christie,** chairman of youth ministry department, San Jose Christian College

Mike got kids to level with him . . . and what they have to say is both fascinating and foundation-shaking. The warning shots have been fired, and if being effective for Christ is what we care about, we need to listen carefully to what is being said—and be prepared to act. *What I Wish My Youth Leader Knew About Youth Ministry* will give youth workers affirmation for hunches about kids they got right and a wake-up call in areas they have misread them. A valuable asset to youth work in this era.

—**Rick Bundschuh,** pastor of Kauai Christian Fellowship, author, *A Youth Ministry Crash Course* and *Magnetic Teaching: making God's Word stick in the lives of your teens*

As I read through *What I Wish My Youth Leader Knew About Youth Ministry,* I was particularly struck by this comment from a Texas tenth grader: "Help us not to be afraid to worship God in front of others." Could it be? Do teenagers really want to worship? What an exciting opportunity to build a confident faith in today's teens. These kinds of eye-opening insights (and others that confirm we're doing some things right) make Mike Nappa's well-organized and information-packed book a top-shelf pick for new and seasoned youth workers alike.

—**Steve Parolini,** editor, *CBA Frontline* magazine

This book is essential for anyone involved in youth ministry. With a wonderful, welcoming approach, Mike takes us on a journey into the hearts and heads of teenagers. The tour may surprise you.

—**Robin Jones Gunn,** teen novelist

It's always refreshing to find a resource that cuts through our assumptions about how things should be and puts the spotlight on how things really are. With this book, Mike Nappa goes straight to the source—the youth themselves—and, pulling no punches, finds out what your youth really think about virtually every aspect of your ministry. This book will help you transform their lives by transforming the ways you minister to them.

—**David Hargrove,** editor-in-chief, *Christian Single* magazine

A NATIONAL SURVEY

What I wish my YOUTH leader knew about youth ministry

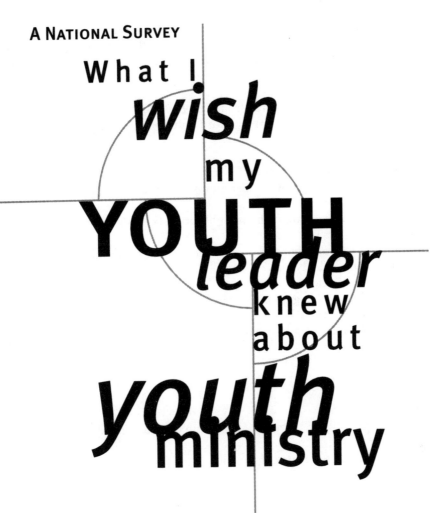

BY MIKE NAPPA

Standard Publishing
Cincinnati, Ohio

Edited by Dale Reeves and Bob Buller
Cover and inside design by Zender and Associates

Library of Congress Cataloging-in-Publication Data:
Nappa, Mike, 1963-
    What I wish my youth leader knew about youth ministry : a national
survey / by Mike Nappa.
    p.   cm.
    Includes bibliographical references.
    ISBN 0-7847-0911-4
    1. Church work with youth. 2. Youth—United States—Interviews.
I.   Title.
BV4447.N327   1999
259'.23—dc21
                           98-45041
                             CIP

The Standard Publishing Company,
Cincinnati, Ohio.
A Division of Standex International Corporation.

06   05   04   03   02   01   00   99
5   4   3   2   1

DEDICATION AND ACKNOWLEDGMENTS

This book is dedicated to Michael Anthony, Ken Garland and Stan Leonard, three men who became both mentors and friends. Thanks for investing in my life and for teaching me that "only people count."

Special thanks also to Dale Reeves, my editor, who believed in this project when everyone else said, "It's just too expensive!" Remind me to buy you lunch sometime.

To Rebecca St. James, my heartfelt thanks for your willingness not only to read this manuscript but also to write the foreword for the book. Your time and contribution are much appreciated.

A debt of gratitude goes out to veteran pollster, Dr. George Barna, a man whom I've met only briefly but whose writings through the years have had a profound effect on me and who was willing to give me helpful advice during the earliest stages of this project.

I owe a huge debt of gratitude to Mike Jones, whose passion for youth ministry made this book possible in the first place.

—M.N.

CONTENTS

FOREWORD

If I were standing face to face with you right now, I would probably give you a big, hearty handshake or a congratulatory pat on the back! Let me explain. . . .

Out on the road the past few years, I have met so many people who work with and love youth, and I respect you guys and gals so much. What you are doing is "on the front lines" and can be really tough. But what an incredible opportunity to be used by God to help shape the coming generation!

I personally have been encouraged and built up spiritually by leaders like you, and if it weren't for them in my life I might not be doing what I'm doing today. I actually came to know Jesus through a youth organization at my church in Australia.

These are just some of the reasons I'm "pumped" about Mike Nappa's book, *What I Wish My Youth Leader Knew About Youth Ministry.* As you can see, I believe very strongly in youth ministry and in what you're doing. You'll find the information in these pages affirming, in that the studies show how significantly you are making a difference. The book also contains a huge amount of practical insights into the hearts and thoughts of my generation. Another reason I am excited about what you are about to read is that it emphasizes an aspect of youth ministry that I think is often underestimated . . . servanthood.

My generation has been told so often that life is about living for ourselves, which is such a devastating lie. Unfortunately, so many have believed it. I feel that one of the ways we can turn away from the curse of selfishness is to serve—to give our lives away. Our Lord and model, Jesus Christ, washed his disciples' feet, then told us to "Love as I have loved you."

I am so challenged by that servant mentality. Through youth group service projects and personal mission trips, God has changed my life. He has shown me the freedom and delight we find in serving others and focusing on their needs above our own. So keep encouraging us as young people to serve. Youth ministry is often a thankless job. On behalf of my generation, I thank you and ask you to please keep on. We need you. Keep encouraging us to live radically for Jesus! Stay close to him and keep loving Jesus more and more.

In his service together,
Rebecca St. James
Acts 20:24

"So my son, throw yourself into this work for Christ. Pass on what you heard . . . concentrate on doing your best for God, work you won't be ashamed of, laying out the truth plain and simple."   2 Timothy 2:1, 15, THE MESSAGE

Introduction

It's Time to Consult the Experts

Three girls in the front row were falling asleep!

I remember the moment vividly—it was a speaker's worst nightmare. (Well, OK, it's not as bad as the dream that finds you preaching in the buff to a crowd of howling junior highers, but it was a close second.)

It was summer 1990. I was speaking at a weekend youth camp in Arizona. As usual, I was excited to tell teenagers about how Jesus could change their lives—both in this world and in the world to come.

My first talk had gotten rave reviews from the leaders. After my second talk, the leaders acted like gold was pouring out with each word I spoke. I must admit I was feeling pretty good about the job I'd done so far. (See how easy it is to let ego get in the way of ministry!)

Then came the third talk—that fateful, ego-deflating, pride-beating, I-can't-believe-I'm-up-here, wake-up-and-smell-the-coffee third talk.

Five minutes into my talk, the girls on the front row started yawning. Then slouching. Then nodding off.

That would have been fine except this was a forty-five minute talk! After ten minutes, I lost the first girl. Her face tilted gently forward, and she slowly entered snoozeland. The second and third girls quickly followed.

I started sweating. I felt a knot of anger begin to form in my stomach. Didn't they know this was great stuff they were missing? Didn't they know no one was supposed to sleep while I was preaching? I spoke louder, emphasizing a key point with a hand-clap that should have awakened the dead.

It didn't.

I called out for responses from the group. I threw in an impromptu interactive illustration, getting other kids out of their seats and moving around. One girl stirred then, but apparently only so she could get more comfortable.

Finally, frustrated and appropriately humbled, I asked a leader to wake up the girls, embarrassing both them and me. I cut the rest of the talk short and went back to my room to sulk.

Looking back now, I see I made a glaring error in my approach to the entire weekend. While preparing my talks, I checked with the adult leaders to find out what was important to the kids in the group, what they were interested in, what they were struggling with, and so on. Then I put together the series of talks based on what the adult leaders told me.

The result? The adults thought I was great; the kids I bored (literally!) to sleep.

A Few Years Later

Now, fast-forward with me a few years to a youth staff meeting in 1996. The topic of the meeting was small groups. To be honest, all of us were trying to figure out how to bolster sagging attendance in our small-group ministries.

"I think we need to be more exciting in our presentation," said one leader.

"We need more publicity about small groups in the midweek meeting," said another.

"Maybe we need to be more aggressive in recruiting kids to come to the groups," added a third.

Then, in an off-the-cuff way, somebody said, "What do you think, Mike? After all, you're the expert."

By this time I had written several youth ministry books, spoken at national conferences, worked for a time as a professional youth pastor, and was now volunteering in the youth department at my church, but it took all of three seconds for me to realize how inadequate I was to answer that question. For all my credentials as an "expert," I was just as lost as everyone else when trying to figure out why the kids weren't coming.

Without really thinking, I replied, "The real experts aren't even in this room right now. If we want to create teen-friendly small groups, we need to consult the experts—our teenagers themselves."

That moment stuck with me, got me thinking about how much of youth ministry in general is run in hit-or-miss fashion. How do we know that kids really want or need the programs we invest so much time in? What makes these programs appealing to teens—or not? We're still using most of the youth ministry methods that originated in the 1970s. Do those methods still work? The only way to find out is to ask the experts—America's teenagers.

So that's what I did.

Asking the Experts

My good friend, Mike Jones, runs a unique organization called Reach

Workcamps. Reach is a nonprofit organization based in Loveland, Colorado that specializes in remodeling and repairing ramshackle homes owned by underprivileged people.

Each summer Reach hosts a series of workcamps at sites all over the nation. Through the years, thousands of teenagers have poured through their program, attending the camp with their youth groups and paying hundreds of dollars for the opportunity to join Reach for a week.

Curious as to what the kids get for their money? They get to sweat, doing physical labor outdoors in scorching heat. They get to sleep on the floors of public schools in poor parts of town, eat cafeteria food each day, hammer, saw, paint, build, repair and generally make life a little easier for others by remodeling homes of underprivileged people.

And the teenagers *love* it. Some come back year after year until they graduate, then sign on as summer interns to work at all the camps!

For the most part these kids are a) Christians, b) involved in a church youth group, and c) motivated to act out the Christian faith by serving others. These are the kinds of kids who make up the core group of teenagers who most consistently attend our youth group meetings, camps, events and more.

I had found my experts.

When I shared with Mike Jones the vision for this book, he generously opened the door to his organization and distributed over eight hundred surveys to teenagers attending a few of his camps. He even donated his office to assist in tabulating the completed surveys!

In the survey, I asked teens to tell me what they wished their youth leader knew about specific areas of youth ministry, and I promised to share their thoughts with you. (A full copy of the survey is found in Appendix 1, page 200.)

Of the more than eight hundred surveys distributed, I culled just over four hundred (403, to be exact) that were complete enough to be counted. After tabulating the totals, I used the results of those surveys to create the basis of the book you're now holding in your hands.

The teenagers were often generous in their responses. Many times they'd write an additional note in the margins, jot down their phone numbers and ask me to call them, underline an answer or add exclamation points.

The young people who responded were literally from all over the nation. States represented in the survey include New York, Pennsylvania, Ohio, Michigan, Indiana, Illinois, Minnesota, Missouri, North Carolina, Georgia, Florida, Kentucky, California, Arizona, Colorado and Texas.

Likewise, these teenagers were involved in a wide variety of Christian traditions. Kids reported that they belonged to churches that were Assemblies of God, Baptist, Bible Churches, Plymouth Brethren, Catholic, Christian Churches, Churches of Christ, Churches of God, Community Churches, Episcopal, Evangelical Congregational, Evangelical Free, Lutheran, Methodist, Presbyterian, Reformed, Vineyard and Independent/Non-Denominational. In all, students from forty-six different church backgrounds participated in the survey.

And for the first time ever, this survey spanned America's two youngest generations, including the now-famous (or is that "infamous"?) GenX upper class (including grades ten to twelve at the time of this survey) and the up-and-coming Millennial/Mosaic under class (grades seven to nine at the time of this survey).

A Brief Look at the Generations

"The game of life is being played differently by each new generation," says pollster George Barna of the Barna Research Group.[1]

Since your youth ministry is currently populated with a blend of two generations, it seems appropriate to briefly look at the current generational trends of these distinct groups.

Generation X (GenX) has become the most talked-about generation the past few years. People of this generation are typically identified as those born between 1961 and 1981.[2] (And yes, even though I'm now ancient in my mid-thirties, I'm still an Xer too. And by my unofficial estimates, about two-thirds of you reading this book are part of GenX as well!)

Briefly, here are some cultural characteristics of GenX teenagers that a few colleagues and I documented in a previous work:[3]

"Most adults prefer a 'black-and-white' world. That means adults like the world around them to be wrapped in nice, neat packages. Everything is either always right or always wrong. Kids are not that way. They prefer to live in a 'gray' world—with no absolutes."

"Today's [GenX] teenagers . . . grew up learning that we can lose wars, that governments can be corrupt, that corporations can be uncaring, and that our planet's natural resources can be depleted. They're more hardened and cynical about life."

"Today's young people value actions far more than they value words."

"Where . . . adults value principles, [GenX] kids value results."

"Adults value what's right; young people value what's *real*."

"Adults see conformity as a sign of unity, but for teenagers, diversity signals unity."

"Adults tend to value relationships only when they're connected to causes they believe in. . . . Kids, however, see life from a flipped perspective. They value relationships more when they're not connected to causes."

"[GenX] kids find meaning in what they can see, hear, touch, taste, and smell."

Sociologists William Strauss and Neil Howe offer this description of GenX as well: "Compared to any other generation born this century, theirs is less cohesive, its experiences wider, its ethnicity more polyglot, and its culture more splintery. Yet all this is their central and collective persona."[4]

With these characteristics in mind, older adults have taken great pleasure in branding GenX with such unpleasant terms as the "lost" generation, a generation of slackers and kids who won't amount to anything. Howe and Strauss report further that, "For the past decade, [GenXers] have been bombarded with study after story after column about how bad they supposedly are. Americans in their teens and twenties, we are told, are consumed with violence, selfishness, greed, bad work habits, and civic apathy."[5]

Unfortunately, this generational slander is all too common. Not long ago, I was leading a Bible study with a small group of GenX teenagers. The topic was the future. As we started discussing what the future may hold in store for them, most of my kids began frowning and looking down. We opened the Scriptures to see what God has in store for believers, and one teen finally said, "That's not what they tell us at school."

Curious, I asked the group what teachers were telling them about their futures. The previously quiet group suddenly sparked with angry conversation. Pointing to one teacher as an example, they reported, "She told us last week that we'd better get used to near-minimum wage jobs because that's all our generation was going to be able to get after we graduate from college."

I personally believe that GenX has much more promise than we get credit for. (With roughly 90 million of us, how could it be otherwise?)[6]

In sharp contrast to GenX, the young people of the Millennial generation (also called the Mosaic generation) have been hailed as the "good" kids. Perceived as a welcome relief from their older sisters and brothers, the Millennial generation is generally thought to include people born from 1982 to the present, as well as future children born until around 2003.[7] When all is said and done, they will probably number about 76 million.[8]

Concerning this up-and-coming generation, Strauss and Howe remark, "From Evangelical Christians to Pentecostals to Muslims, many of today's new religious currents revolve around parishioners' protective urges toward small children."[9]

Howe and Strauss further report that this positive sentiment toward the Millennial generation is showing itself in increased parental involvement in kids' lives, record numbers of "stay-at-home dads," and movements such as the Muslim and Promise Keepers' "million man" marches on Washington.[10]

Howe and Strauss offer more insight into the characteristics of this fourteenth American generation by describing them as follows:[11]

"MILLENNIAL GENERATION. Cute. Cheerful. Scoutlike. Wanted."

"Not since the early 1900s have older generations moved so quickly to . . . implant civic virtue in a new crop of youngsters."

"The goal [adults have for Millennial kids] aims at the nurture of what some are calling a 'new generation' whose excellence Americans hope to celebrate when the Millennium arrives."

"Fueling this adult mission toward the Millennial generation is palpable (mainly Boom[er]) disappointment in how the 13th [GenX] is turning out."

"First wave Millennials are riding a powerful crest of concern, dating back to the early 1980s, over the American childhood environment."

"Where [GenX] kids were best known as latchkeys, throwaways, boomerangs, and other terms implying that adults would just as soon have them disappear, Millennials have so far been perceived very differently—as kids whom adults wish to guard with dutiful care."

"Someday, Boomers hope, Millennials will build according to great ideals their parents can only envision, act on vital issues their parents can only ponder. These children are not being raised to explore the inner world, but instead to achieve and excel at the outer."

"Others speculate that [Millennial kids] might grow up to be great scientists who can solve the riddle of cancer, great engineers who can protect the environment, and great producers who can put an end to world hunger."

The jury is still out on this latest generation. Are Millennial kids *that* different—and therefore "better" (as perceived by Boomers)—than their GenX siblings? Will Millennials indeed be the redeeming force they're being told they are? Will GenX cast a larger-than-expected shadow of influence on their Millennial kid brothers and sisters? And if they do, will that be a positive or negative thing?

Hard to say, but one thing we know for sure is this: Millennial kids now make up more than half of most American youth groups.

The unique timing of this is excellent. At this special juncture in history, we can actually encounter *two* distinct generations in our youth groups. That allows us, through the grandparenting of faith, to stretch the impact of our ministries more than double the length, impacting not only today and tomorrow, but several lifetimes of tomorrows in American churches as well.

For that reason, I felt it was important—even imperative—to include both GenXers and Millennial kids in this survey. To the best of my knowledge, at the time this book was written no other work on youth ministry had yet benefited from surveys of the Millennial generation.

That means that you and I, together through this book, can get a first look at how Millennials are beginning to influence our ministry environments and plan accordingly. We can glimpse what works for both Xers and Millennials, and then we can tailor our methods to be effective today, tomorrow and for many years to come.

A Few Things You Should Know About the Survey

Now, enough about the generations. Let's talk just a bit more about the survey, because there are a few last things you should know.

First, you'll quickly notice that not all of the survey percentages add up to 100 percent. Sometimes they're more, sometimes they're less. No, it's not because I flunked math in high school! Rather, it's because I gave respondents a little leeway in how they answered survey questions.

Several questions (such as queries about worship, group games and events) allowed youth group members to choose more than one answer. In those cases, the totals for each answer obviously go over 100 percent. Other questions (such as those about Sunday school and midweek meetings) were not always applicable, so teenagers were allowed to leave them blank. In those cases, the totals could be less than 100 percent.

The margin of error for our survey is ±5%.

Finally, when survey percentages included fractions (i.e., 33 1/3 percent), I rounded off to the nearest full percentage point. In those cases the totals will sometimes be a bit less or a bit more than 100 percent, depending on how the rounding went.

As part of the survey, I also asked kids if they'd be willing to participate in follow-up phone interviews to talk about the survey questions. Many, many young people (about double what I'd expected!) were willing—even eager—to do this.

For the sake of time, I limited the follow-up interviews to twenty kids chosen randomly from the survey population. The thoughts and insights those kids had to share turn up in the pages of this book.

On a clerical note, you'll notice that I often refer to the kids in the survey as "teenagers." Truth is, all the seventh graders and many of the eighth graders are still pre-teens. However, since youth ministry is generally characterized as a ministry to "teenagers," I assumed you wouldn't mind if I blurred the terms a bit here.

Finally, I wanted to gauge, roughly, how the attitudes of the teenagers themselves matched with our perceptions as youth leaders of their attitudes. So, I contacted about twenty of my friends who are either currently active in youth ministry or have substantial youth ministry experience in the recent past. I asked each of these leaders to take the survey, answering questions the way they thought an average teenager would answer. Comparing these adult surveys with the teen results was sometimes eye-opening, sometimes encouraging and always interesting. You'll see some of these leaders' opinions in this book as well.

Now, perhaps most importantly, please realize that this survey and this book deal only with *methods*, not the *message*, of youth ministry. That's so important, I'm going to say it again:

This survey and this book deal only with *methods*, not the *message*, of youth ministry.

The message of your ministry should be the same one that Paul preached thousands of years ago: Christ, and him crucified (see 1 Corinthians 1:23, 24). Nowhere in this book will you find me suggesting otherwise, so please don't try to misconstrue any thoughts in this book as meaning we should substitute *anything* for the gospel of Jesus Christ. To do so would invalidate any reason for ministering to teenagers in the first place.

That said, you should also know that I believe any *method* of ministry is subject to being changed, improved or abandoned as ministry conditions warrant. Our job as youth leaders is to maximize our impact on young people, for Christ's sake. If that means redefining Sunday school, holding midnight meetings or wearing bananas on our heads for the next twenty years, then we ought to do it—or at least consider doing it.

That's what this book is about. A chance for us to consider the methods that will help us maximize our presentation of the message—and, in the process, change the world one student at a time.

Let's Get Started!

Now, before you dive into the rest of this book, I want to share with you a story I once heard. I'm told it's a true story, but I can't document that for you. Still, whether it's fact or fable, the point is the same.

The story goes something like this . . .

A man went to a busy office to apply for a job as a telegraph operator. He was running late and was dismayed when he entered the reception area. Nearly every seat was filled with hopeful applicants, all waiting their turns to walk through the door to the adjoining interview room where company executives would choose one person to fill the position.

All around, the regular workers busily went about their duties. Secretaries typed, messengers delivered and in the background the steady Morse-code beat of the telegraph rang through the walls.

The man contemplated leaving, but he really needed this job. So, after a moment's hesitation, he took a seat near the far wall. For several minutes, no one moved, waiting out the time. Then, suddenly, the man jumped out of his seat and strode confidently through the door of the interview room.

Other applicants clucked their tongues in disapproval after the door closed. Surely a person with the audacity to interrupt the company execs would be tossed out on his ear in moments. When the door opened again only five minutes later, they knew they were right.

But they were wrong. "You can all go home," announced the company's president. Then, slapping the audacious man on the shoulder, he added, "We've found our man."

Some of the other applicants started to protest but were quickly quieted when the president explained. "Listen closely to the telegraph sounds tapping through these walls," he said. "Then you'll know why we've hired this man." With that, he closed the door.

Straining their ears, the others finally tuned in the sounds of the telegraph and took time to interpret the Morse code coming through the walls. Here's what they heard:

"If you hear this, come in the interview room now. The job is yours."

Like the executives at this company, our teenagers are sending us messages to help us succeed in our ministry to them. And like the applicants in this story, we can choose to listen or to ignore what they're saying to us. I say we walk through the door.

Care to join me?

"How, then, can they call on the one
they have not believed in?
And how can they believe
in the one of whom they have not heard?
And how can they hear
without someone preaching to them?"
– Romans 10:14

Chapter 1

What I Wish My Youth Leader Knew About . . .

Youth Talks/Sermons

It's a classic in the lore of fairy tales. It seems there once lived a disagreeable and greedy old woman who had two daughters. The older was just as disagreeable and greedy as the mother— and, of course, the mother's favorite. The younger was good and kind.

Much like poor Cinderella, this younger daughter was made to work at all kinds of chores the other two women in the family considered beneath them. One fateful day (because there's always a "fateful day" in fairy tales), the younger daughter went to draw from the spring and met a poverty-stricken woman begging for water. In a fit of compassion, she not only drew a cup of water but held the cup for the destitute woman.

You guessed it. The poor beggar was actually a fairy in disguise. As a reward for the girl, the fairy proclaimed, "At every word you speak, either a flower or a jewel shall come out of your mouth." From that point on, every time the girl spoke, a dizzying array of diamonds, pearls and roses dripped extravagantly from her lips.

> "The average attention span among teenagers today is estimated at six to eight minutes. . . . The average sermon lasts 31 minutes."
>
> —Dr. George Barna[1]

Needless to say, the mother and older daughter were quite jealous. So they decided the older sister should go to the spring and do the same thing. That older girl had scarcely arrived at the spring when a beautiful princess came out of the woods and asked for a drink. Thinking she had only to serve a beggar woman, this older sister refused and spoke rudely to the future queen.

You guessed it again. Same fairy, different disguise. As a punishment for the older daughter's greed and unkindness, the fairy proclaimed, "At every word you speak, toads and serpents shall come out of your mouth."

So, from that day forward, everyone longed to hear the younger daughter speak and thus be showered with riches but dreaded hearing the older daughter because it meant a downpour of warty toads and poisonous snakes.

Now, I know this isn't a theologically correct fairy tale, but I must admit to wishing at times that a speaker's words could be so easily—and quickly—judged. Imagine the difference it would make in our youth talks if we could gauge the value of our words simply by what came out along with them!

"Let's see," we might say afterward, "That's seventy-two diamonds, and only eleven snakes. Not bad! Not bad at all."

Or maybe we'd start off a talk with fourteen straight toads, then wisely end the sermon there and spend time praying instead.

Or even better, and less messy, what if we could put on a miraculous pair of "speaker's glasses" that allowed us to see (in thought balloons) what our kids were thinking during the time we spoke? We might see comments such as . . .

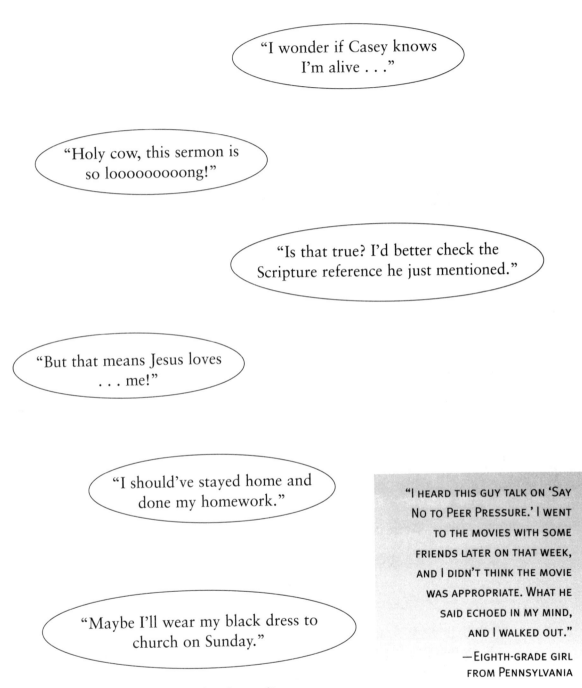

"I wonder if Casey knows I'm alive . . ."

"Holy cow, this sermon is so loooooooooong!"

"Is that true? I'd better check the Scripture reference he just mentioned."

"But that means Jesus loves . . . me!"

"I should've stayed home and done my homework."

"Maybe I'll wear my black dress to church on Sunday."

"I HEARD THIS GUY TALK ON 'SAY NO TO PEER PRESSURE.' I WENT TO THE MOVIES WITH SOME FRIENDS LATER ON THAT WEEK, AND I DIDN'T THINK THE MOVIE WAS APPROPRIATE. WHAT HE SAID ECHOED IN MY MIND, AND I WALKED OUT."

—EIGHTH-GRADE GIRL FROM PENNSYLVANIA

Unfortunately (or fortunately, depending on your perspective!), we're not gifted with supernatural abilities to evaluate the sermons, devotions and lectures we deliver regularly to our kids. So how can we discover what our kids really want and need in a youth talk?

We ask them.

Synchronize Your Watches, Please

There are a hundred different questions you could ask teenagers about sermons, but since I wanted you to actually read this book, I decided to focus on three main areas: desired sermon length, desired sermon methods and desired sermon content. Let's start with sermon length.

Imagine that you're a teenager in your youth group. What time length would you (as a teenager) think is best for a typical youth talk? Under fifteen minutes? Between fifteen and thirty minutes? Maybe thirty to forty-five minutes? More?

"POOR PREACHING IS RESPONSIBLE FOR A LOT OF POOR PRESENTATIONS OF THE GOSPEL AND THE LOSS OF A HOST OF OPPORTUNITIES TO LEAD PEOPLE INTO THE KINGDOM OF GOD."
—ANTHONY CAMPOLO[2]

Whenever I raise this subject with other youth leaders, they almost always shake their heads and say, "Kids today just don't have the attention span to allow me to dig deeply into a sermon topic."

I remember one time in particular. I was involved in a junior high midweek meeting for a well-known church in southern California. Each week, more than two hundred seventh and eighth graders spent a few hours with us at "Mania!" Occasionally, other youth pastors would drop in to observe our program.

After one evening's meeting, a visiting youth pastor came up to me incredulous that: 1) we'd slotted forty-five minutes for a sermon, and 2) the kids seemed attentive the whole time.

"In my group," he said, "we could never do that. In fact, we've cut back our talk time to only ten or fifteen minutes. We spend the rest of the time in games, singing and crowdbreakers."

Checking my survey of youth leaders for this book, I discovered that more than one-third of us (35%) agrees with that youth ministry veteran and think limiting a youth talk to under fifteen minutes is best.

Still, a healthy percentage of us are willing to stretch that sermon time to thirty minutes. Fifty-five percent of those surveyed think a talk for teenagers is optimum when it falls between the fifteen- and thirty-minute marks. Almost none of us are willing to go beyond that. One in ten would risk thirty to forty-five minutes, but no one surveyed would subject kids to a talk longer than forty-five minutes.

How does that compare with what the teenagers themselves think? Let's find out.

Just over half (51%) of seventh through twelfth graders join the majority of youth leaders in recommending that a youth talk be limited to between fifteen and thirty minutes. That's significant, because it indicates we're close to making an accurate gauge of what teenagers will be most receptive to in terms of sermon length.

> "YOU LEARN THROUGH ASKING QUESTIONS. I WAS VERY MUCH UNDER THE IMPRESSION THAT WHEN YOU ASKED QUESTIONS, THAT MEANT YOU WERE DOUBTING AND THEREFORE NOT 'WALKING THE WALK' OR 'TALKING THE TALK.' [I THOUGHT] IT WAS WRONG TO ASK QUESTIONS. IN MY OWN LIFE, I'M LEARNING THAT SOMETHING THE LORD WANTS US TO DO IS ASK QUESTIONS. . . . THAT'S HOW WE LEARN. GOD IS NOT INTIMIDATED BY OUR QUESTIONS! THAT'S ONE THING THAT'S BEEN ON MY HEART TO COMMUNICATE TO KIDS."
>
> —STEPHEN MASON, GUITARIST & VOCALIST FOR JARS OF CLAY[3]

However, from that point on, it seems we may be underestimating our kids. Although 35 percent (one in three) of the youth leaders suggest a youth talk of fifteen minutes or less, only about one of ten teenagers (11%) would request that. In fact (and contrary to popular belief), if we decide to deviate from the fifteen- to thirty-minute rule, more than one-fourth (27%) of our kids would rather we go longer instead of shorter, suggesting we take up to forty-five minutes to deliver our message.

Then, of course, there are those hardy souls, teenagers for whom "pew time" is sacred. These kids number about 10 percent of our groups, and of that number, 80 percent (or 8% of the whole group) say we should take up to an hour. The other 20 percent (2% of the whole) will sit there as long as we're willing to talk, suggesting we go "more than an hour" in delivering our talks.

"HOW LONG DO YOU THINK IS BEST FOR A TYPICAL YOUTH TALK OR SERMON?"

	YOUTH LEADER RESPONSES	7TH-12TH GRADE RESPONSES
Less than 15 minutes	35%	11%
Between 15 - 30 minutes	55%	51%
Between 30 - 45 minutes	10%	27%
Between 45 - 60 minutes	0%	8%
More than an hour	0%	2%

And During the Sermon?

If the optimum youth talk runs about thirty minutes, then what should we be doing to keep kids' attention during that precious time?

It has been my observation that lecture is by far our most-used method. Is it working? Sadly, no. Only 4 percent of our kids said "lecture only" was most effective in helping them learn from a sermon. In fact, youth group members rated this method *dead last* in effectiveness, just behind "formal Scripture readings."

The funny thing is, youth leaders rated this method dead last (in a tie with formal Scripture readings) as well, which raises the question: If kids don't like it, and *we know* kids don't like it, why do we insist on using lecture so heavily in our teaching methods?

"Mike," you say, "that's someone else's group. I don't use lecture too much here. My kids like my lectures, anyway. And besides, the lecture method is what they taught me in seminary—and the method my professors used to teach me about youth ministry!"

> "EXCELLENCE AND PROFESSIONALISM ARE 'PERFORMANCE STRATEGIES' THAT APPEAL TO THE LATE BUILDERS AND EARLY BOOMERS. AMONG THE BUSTERS [GENXERS] HOWEVER, THE KEYS ARE RELEVANCE, GENUINENESS AND AUTHENTICITY. THEY ARE MORE INTERESTED IN EXPERIENCING A SINCERE AND HONEST PRESENTATION THAT RAISES MEANINGFUL QUESTIONS THAN A POLISHED, WELL-REHEARSED SPEECH THAT PROVIDES ALL THE ANSWERS. . . . THE COMMUNICATIONS STRATEGY THAT HAS MOST EFFECTIVELY OVERCOME THEIR AVERSION TO MORAL ABSOLUTES HAS BEEN THE INTELLIGENT USE OF STORIES AS THE MEANS OF CONVEYING TRUTH."
> —DR. GEORGE BARNA[4]

Pardon my frankness when I say that I think we're deluding ourselves into thinking too much lecture is only a problem in "someone else's group." Perhaps it's time some of us admit lecture is boring our kids too, and at least try to do something about it.

So if lecture leaves our kids cold, what should we be doing?

Well, our kids have spoken on this topic and their answer is that, well, *they'd* like to speak more!

By far the number one learning method teenagers desire is discussion. We all know kids like to talk, but did you know that your kids like to talk about your sermon? And not only do they like this kind of interaction, they learn more from it too.

Christian education experts, Thom and Joani Schultz, put it this way, "In an interactive classroom, the teacher poses the question, then asks students to discuss the question in pairs or foursomes. *Every* individual is involved. Everybody works on problem-solving. Every person learns."[6]

One survey respondent agreed with the Schultzes. Describing why a sermon on Lazarus's resurrection had made a lasting impact, she said simply, "It was memorable because [during the sermon] everyone talked and had something to say."

Your teenagers also rate your stories and sermon-focused skits very highly, rating these two methods as numbers two and three, respectively. Girls are evenly divided about whether skits or stories are better, ranking both in a tie for second. Guys, by a healthy 11 percentage points, prefer stories over skits, which influences the overall totals and causes stories to be ranked second.

Interestingly, although each grade level ranked discussion, stories and skits as their top three choices of sermon methods, the age groups differed on how much importance they gave these categories. For example, both seventh and eighth graders rated stories as their most-desired method, ranking it ahead of the overall winner, discussion, by significant margins.

By contrast, nearly two-thirds (62%) of tenth graders desired discussion, with less than half (44%) asking for stories. Juniors and seniors also rated discussion as their method of choice, ranking skits in the number two slot, and letting stories fall in at a close third.

"I LEARN MOST FROM A YOUTH TALK/SERMON WHEN IT INCLUDES . . ."

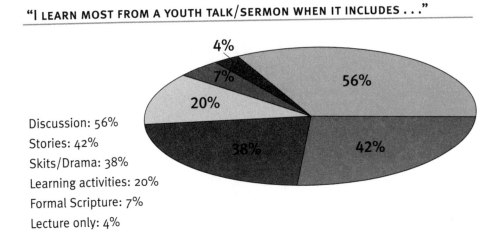

Discussion: 56%
Stories: 42%
Skits/Drama: 38%
Learning activities: 20%
Formal Scripture: 7%
Lecture only: 4%

DESIRED SERMON METHODS, BY GRADE

	7TH	8TH	9TH	10TH	11TH	12TH
Discussion	40%	46%	58%	62%	51%	55%
Stories	47%	58%	45%	44%	38%	38%
Skits/Drama	40%	38%	42%	33%	42%	39%
Learning activities	20%	8%	27%	20%	16%	20%
Formal Scripture readings	13%	13%	3%	8%	9%	6%
Lecture only	13%	4%	5%	4%	4%	2%

Sermon Content

Now that we know what kids want in terms of length and method, we have to wonder what they desire in terms of content.

When I was a youth pastor several years ago, one of my volunteers came to me with this valid complaint. "Mike," she said, "why is every talk we give to our kids focused on some current teen topic? I mean, how many times can we preach sermons on sex, drugs, peer pressure and the like? Really, why can't we sometimes just start with the Bible and preach a sermon from there, instead of vice versa?"

So, at the next open slot, I scheduled a series that was exegetical in nature, starting with a passage

> "AT THE BEGINNING OF YOUR TALK THERE OCCURS A RARE OPPORTUNITY THAT MAY NOT PRESENT ITSELF IN QUITE THE SAME WAY AT ANY OTHER TIME. IN THOSE FIRST FEW SECONDS YOU HAVE AN ATTENTIVE AUDIENCE. AND IN THOSE FIRST FEW SECONDS THE AUDIENCE DECIDES WHETHER OR NOT YOU ARE WORTH LISTENING TO. THOSE FIRST 50 WORDS ARE THE MOST IMPORTANT WORDS YOU WILL SPEAK."
>
> —KEN DAVIS[7]

of Scripture and then working our way through it to find applicable life lessons.

It was a hit. Kids liked it, and we felt like we were providing good biblical content. In fact, it was such a good thing, we tried it again. This time, however, it flopped, boring the kids and dragging on too long.

So which works best? Topical sermons or exegetical sermons that apply Scripture to real-life situations? Would you believe that the answer is both?

At first glance, it would appear teenagers want to hear only topical sermons. After all, they did vote that their preference by a two-to-one margin. But it's worthwhile to note that one out of three youth group members still prefers an exegetical lesson.

> INTERVIEWER:
> "TELL ME ABOUT THE MOST MEMORABLE SERMON YOU'VE EVER HEARD."
>
> MALE TENTH GRADER FROM GEORGIA:
> "I DON'T THINK THERE IS ONE."

That means that although we're more likely to have success reaching teenagers with topical youth talks, our kids are still open to receiving basic instruction directly from the pages of God's Word. It's a win-win situation for all involved.

Unfortunately, this is another area where we as youth leaders are out of balance with the teenagers we serve. Fully 85 percent (or nearly nine out of ten) of the youth leaders I surveyed felt that teens would prefer topical sermons over Scripture passage-based lessons. Although we're right in predicting the majority, it appears we've given that majority perception a bit too much emphasis when preparing the content of our messages to kids. A more balanced approach seems appropriate instead.

TOPICAL VS. EXEGETICAL YOUTH TALKS/SERMONS?

	RESPONSES	
	YOUTH LEADER	7TH-12TH GRADE
Real-life topics, then apply appropriate Scripture	85%	69%
Scripture first, then apply to real-life situations	15%	30%

Chapter Summary and Observations

The optimum amount of time for a youth talk is between fifteen and thirty minutes, although a significant number of kids are willing to listen for up to forty-five minutes (assuming the content is worthwhile). What does that mean for us?

"WITH THE LITTLE YOUTH TALKS YOU GIVE, REMEMBER TO BE ABLE TO RELATE IT TO LIFE SO YOUR KIDS CAN REMEMBER IT."

—EIGHTH-GRADE PRESBYTERIAN

First, we should be time-conscious speakers. We need to plan our talks to fit within that fifteen- to forty-five-minute range, and mark ahead of time the sections we can cut if time is running short.

Secondly, we need to remember to recapture our kids' attention periodically throughout the sermon. Even fifteen minutes can be extremely unbearable if a speaker simply drones on and on without giving listeners a reason to pay attention. (Imagine how boring a fifteen-minute reading of scientific formulas would be!) We need to be ready about every ten minutes or so to use an attention-getting hook, such as a change in teaching method, to call back the straying lambs in our audience.

Third, we can't be afraid to take our time—weeks in fact! If we're exploring a subject that requires deeper study, we need to give ourselves permission to spread it out over several meetings.

If you hit that thirty-minute mark and realize you've gone only partway through point two, try saying this: "I've got much more to share about this topic, but rather than keep you here any longer, I'll finish this next time." By doing this, you will accomplish three things: 1) You will give your topic the time it deserves; 2) You will show sensitivity to the time concerns of your students; and 3) You will (hopefully) whet kids' appetites for the rest of the material that's to come.

When it comes to speaking methods, teenagers rate these as their top three choices: discussion, stories and skits.

It's important to note that all three of these methods garnered significant support from teenagers. With that in mind, we should make an effort first of all to offer variety in our teaching time. There's no law against including discussion in your talk one week, a skit the next and a story or two in both.

We also need to redefine our roles as bearers of Christ's message to teenagers. Instead of acting as the all-knowing lecturer (which was appropriate years ago, but not so appropriate today), we will increase our effectiveness if we can view ourselves as learning facilitators instead. As facilitators, we can then easily transition from a lecture segment, to a discussion time, to a skit, to a learning activity. We will expand our limits and increase attentiveness at the same time.

That said, we can't deny the importance of creating opportunities for discussion. This is probably the easiest and most effective method we can use during a sermon. Make a point, pause to allow teenagers to talk to each other about that point, then have volunteers share the results of their discussions. When this happens, it allows kids to receive the message, think about the message, verbalize the message and thus crystallize the message in their minds—all within a few minutes' time.

Don't miss the opportunity to tell a good yarn, either. Stories are fun to hear and even more fun to tell. Read a lot, and share what you read with your kids. Pay attention to the little dramas that happen in life—in line at the grocery store, at the beach, at the high school football game—and relate memorable moments to your audience.

While you're at it, cultivate a dramatic flair—or at least form a skit troupe out of kids at the church. When you're preparing a sermon, think of a brief skit that also makes the point. Then use teen actors and the skit to introduce your talk, to reinforce a point smack-dab in the middle of your talk or to drive home your message at the end.

Roughly two-thirds of teenagers prefer sermons that are topical in nature, while the remaining one-third would rather hear an exegetical talk.

As a rule, then, it'd probably work well to preach topical sermons two-thirds of the time, and sprinkle in exegetical talks from time to time as well. For example, if you're planning fifty talks in a given year, make thirty-three of them topical and seventeen of them Scripture-originated.

For Personal Reflection

Take a few moments now to process your own reaction to the information in this chapter. Use these questions to help spark your thinking:

- *Which of the survey results discussed in this chapter was most memorable for you? Why do you suppose that was true?*

- *Based on the information you just read, how would you rate the youth talks your group hears (whether by you or another speaker)? In what areas are you doing well? In what areas would you like to improve?*

- *What's one change you could make in the next thirty days to maximize the effectiveness of your youth group's teaching time?*

> "COME, LET US BOW DOWN IN WORSHIP,
> LET US KNEEL BEFORE THE LORD OUR MAKER;
> FOR HE IS OUR GOD AND WE ARE
> THE PEOPLE OF HIS PASTURE,
> THE FLOCK UNDER HIS CARE."
> —PSALM 95:6, 7

Chapter 2

WHAT I WISH MY YOUTH LEADER KNEW ABOUT . . .

GROUP SINGING AND WORSHIP

The servant didn't know quite what to think. After all, it's not often you find your employer with tears streaming down his face—especially in the year 1741. But when this servant went in to see his employer, George F. Handel, that's what happened.

Handel, a composer, had been working on a new oratorio to be called *Messiah*. The lyrics, compiled by Charles Jennens, all came straight from Scripture and told the story of Jesus. It was Handel's job to compose the music to accompany those words.

What he didn't know was that his "work" would soon turn into worship.

For twenty-four days Handel worked, barely taking time to eat or sleep. The project consumed him, drew his soul like none other had. As he poured over the Scriptures and added the musical backdrop, he found himself transfixed by the beauty in the story of Jesus.

> "IT [WORSHIP] BRINGS US TOGETHER, IN A SENSE. WE'RE ALL DOING ONE THING AT ONE TIME, AND THAT'S PRAISING GOD."
> —TENTH-GRADE MALE FROM TEXAS

45

Finally he reached the end of the oratorio and, with trembling hand, began to score the finale, a song simply called "The Hallelujah Chorus." Before he could reach the conclusion, however, he was so overwhelmed by God's presence that he began to sob uncontrollably. And that was when his servant came in the room and found him.

Handel could offer only one explanation for his behavior. He'd been so powerfully caught in worship, he couldn't contain himself. "I think I did see all Heaven before me," he said with awe, "and the great God himself!"[2]

The story doesn't end there. A few short years later, Handel's *Messiah* was being performed for an illustrious audience that included the king of England himself. When the time came for the finale, the king was so moved by the worshipful spirit of "The Hallelujah Chorus" that he too had to respond. Instead of breaking down in tears, though, the king stood in reverent respect for God—and remained standing through the entire song!

It was customary in England at that time for people to stand any time their king stood, so when others in the audience saw the king rise to his feet, they did likewise. As a result, the entire audience stood until the song reached its end.[3]

It's been more than 250 years since Handel composed this song and since the king of England responded to it, but "The Hallelujah Chorus" still moves people to worship. It's been re-recorded hundreds of times, appears in movies (remember *Home Alone?*) and in Christmas specials, and has been sung by a large gathering of contemporary Christian music luminaries—twice!

And chances are, if your church sang it this past Christmas season, everyone in the congregation stood for the song, continuing a tradition begun by the king of England two centuries ago.

Too Much Worship?

If you haven't guessed it already, I tell you this story to make a point: Worship is powerful—powerful enough to change people from within, powerful enough to renew the brokenhearted, powerful enough to impact the teenagers in your youth group forever.

Keith Anderson is chaplain at Bethel College and author of *What They Don't Always Teach You at a Christian College* (InterVarsity Press). Listen to what he reports about the effects of worship on his campus:

"Worship which is rich, lively and welcoming—it helps students learn to love the God who loves them. The hottest thing in Christian colleges today is contemporary worship. We have over one thousand students who meet every Sunday night in our gym for a student-led time of worship with guitars, drums, pianos, keyboards and lots of joyful enthusiasm. A thousand of our students meet because they know that Vespers is the place to be!"[4]

> "GOD IS THE RELENTLESS LOVER. OUR HEARTS WILL NEVER BE SATISFIED UNTIL THEY ARE FILLED WITH HIM. WE WILL NEVER BE ABLE TO FULLY LOVE OTHERS UNTIL WE ARE ABSORBED IN A DAILY ROMANCE WITH GOD."
> —ROBIN JONES GUNN[5]

It's true that students are drawn to worship, but could it be we put too much emphasis on this aspect of our ministry to teenagers? When I asked teenagers that question, they responded emphatically—and their answer was "No!"

Of all the teenagers I surveyed, barely 3 percent reported that their youth group regularly spends "too much" time in worship. By contrast, the other 97 percent reported the time their youth groups spend in worship is "about right" (79%) or "not enough" (18%).

It's encouraging to discover that just over three-fourths of our kids are satisfied with the worship prompts that we provide. Good job for us! What's interesting to note, however, is that nearly one in five of the students to whom we minister has a craving for even more time spent in worship.

When I approached the data, I expected to see some kind of easily recognizable pattern among kids' desire for more time in worship. I half expected younger youth group members not to have a whole lot of interest in worship and older ones to feel a deeper need for it—or vice versa.

Surprisingly, there was no real pattern. Seventh graders reported the most longing for more time in worship, with one in three saying their current time expenditures were "not enough." But then eighth graders—with whom the seventh grade typically worships—rated a desire for more worship comparatively low, with only one in eight requesting it. Likewise, one out of every four eleventh graders expressed a wish for more worship time, whereas that number dropped to only one out of six students in the twelfth grade.

> "[REGULAR WORSHIP EXPERIENCES] ARE VERY IMPORTANT FOR A YOUTH GROUP. THEY GET TO PRAISE GOD AND TALK TO GOD. I THINK PRAISE IS IMPORTANT FOR A YOUTH GROUP."
>
> —EIGHTH-GRADE FEMALE FROM PENNSYLVANIA

I'd love to be able to make more sense out of those survey results for you, but to be honest I can only guess. Perhaps worship is more meaningful depending on personal life circumstances that vary from teenager to teenager. Perhaps the seventh and eleventh graders in this survey face fewer life stresses than their eighth and twelfth grade counterparts, who are anticipating graduation from junior high/middle school and graduation from high school into adulthood. Or perhaps God has simply chosen to meet these kids in a special way during worship.

Regardless of who desires more time in worship, however, it's apparent that our teenagers—all grades—value time spent praising God.

When I asked a few kids in follow-up interviews to share why teenagers desire worship experiences in youth group, here's what they had to say:

INTERVIEWER: "WHAT'S THE BEST ADVICE YOU COULD GIVE TO A YOUTH PASTOR?" TENTH GRADER FROM TEXAS: "HELP US NOT TO BE AFRAID TO WORSHIP GOD IN FRONT OF OTHERS . . . [BECAUSE WE] MIGHT BE AFRAID OF PRAYING AND WHAT FRIENDS MIGHT THINK."

"There's a lot of involvement [in worship]. You don't just sit there and do nothing. You're really involved."—Tenth-grade male from Georgia

"[Worship] is a different way to praise God than just *talking* about it. I love to sing, especially with my friends."—Tenth-grade female from Michigan

That love of singing comes out strongly in this survey, and in keeping with tradition, singing is the form of worship we youth leaders are most likely to use as a worship prompt for our kids.

"ON THE WHOLE, THE TIME OUR YOUTH GROUP REGULARLY SPENDS IN WORSHIP IS . . ."

About right	79%
Not enough	18%
Too much	3%

NUMBER OF TEENS WHO DESIRE MORE TIME SPENT IN WORSHIP, BY GRADE:

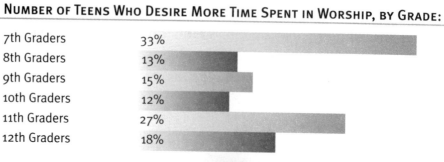

7th Graders	33%
8th Graders	13%
9th Graders	15%
10th Graders	12%
11th Graders	27%
12th Graders	18%

Let's Talk About Singing

Nearly two-thirds (63%) of the teenagers who took this survey rated group singing as the form of worship they like most—which is good because that's also the form of worship in which a majority of kids (57%) say their group most often participates.

So what are we singing? Let's explore.

Not long ago, I was the songbook team coordinator for a now-published collection of youth group worship songs. As part of the research for that songbook, I surveyed youth leaders, studied current youth songbooks, and held a focus group or two to talk directly to youth leaders about what songs they wanted to share with their kids.

An overwhelming majority asked for what I call "old standard" praise songs—that is, classic songs such as "Pharaoh, Pharaoh," "I am a C" and "Do Lord." Many also decried the loss of hymns in youth group worship time—but not one of those people was doing something about it by including hymns in their own groups.

> FROM A CARTOON BY DOUG HALL:
> "LATER ANALYSIS CONCLUDED THAT 'WORSHIP ON ICE' FAILED BECAUSE IT REQUIRED GIFTS NOT LISTED IN 1 CORINTHIANS 12."[6]

Then one youth leader insisted that any good songbook had to include a few then-current hits from contemporary Christian music (CCM). When I reported that to my boss—a veteran youth worker herself—she was mystified. "Do youth groups really sing those?" she asked. "They seem too hard for the average youth leader to play and too complicated for the average teenager to sing."

To her credit, she was at least willing to consider the idea. So I visited this youth pastor's youth group and watched as he led kids in energetic versions of Audio Adrenaline's "Big House," Steven Curtis Chapman's "King of the Jungle" and Newsboys' "Not Ashamed." Not only did the kids know the songs by heart—they couldn't wait to shout out their praise in these tunes!

Later, near the end of the meeting, the youth pastor put on a CCM ballad to introduce a prayer time. These same kids who had danced with rowdy abandon to "Big House" now knelt in worshipful prayer to the strains of that song.

I walked away from that meeting thinking that when it comes to the songs we present for worship, perhaps we youth leaders are too stuck on the old familiar tunes we heard when we were kids.

Hymns, Praise Songs or CCM?

That songbook came out, and it did include a few CCM hits alongside a plethora of "old standards." The next question is, "Which songs should you choose for your group?"

Well, for starters it's true that most teenagers don't get anything from hymns (the "old standards" for our parents!). Only 5 percent of those surveyed marked "hymns" when asked the question, "Which do you like best during a time of group singing?" (It's worth noting, though, that when I asked youth leaders the same question, exactly 0 percent chose hymns.)

Youth leaders overwhelmingly assumed that teenagers like "singing mostly praise songs" best. Only one in four indicated that teens might like CCM tunes best.

In this area, our prevalent perceptions are both right and wrong. Truth is, teenagers *do* like singing praise songs during worship—and they like it a lot. In fact, 49 percent of the young people surveyed—nearly half of those teenagers—rated praise songs as their favorites. In this context, we seem to be doing a good job of providing meaningful music to worship by.

> "THERE'S A SONG BY BLUES TRAVELER CALLED 'A HUNDRED YEARS.' IN THE SONG, THEY SAY THAT WHATEVER YOU'RE DOING IN LIFE WON'T MEAN A THING IN 100 YEARS. BUT, I THINK WHAT WE'RE DOING WILL MATTER!"
>
> —BEN CISSELL, DRUMMER FOR AUDIO ADRENALINE[7]

Curious how many teenagers rated using contemporary Christian music during worship time as best? Forty-seven percent—again almost half of all kids, and only two percentage points fewer than the number of people who chose praise songs.

In reality, only seven students (out of 403) made up the difference in these two totals. Generally speaking it's the guys in our groups who like CCM in worship the most, with a small majority of male respondents selecting that choice. Girls take the opposite view, however, and choose praise songs by a slim majority.

To me, this strong showing of contemporary Christian music in these numbers indicates that perhaps that youth leader who insisted on including CCM songs in a youth ministry songbook had a good pulse on what is meaningful for teenagers today.

WHICH DO TEENAGERS LIKE BEST DURING A TIME OF GROUP SINGING?

	TEENAGERS' CHOICES	YOUTH LEADERS' CHOICES
Singing mostly hymns	5%	0%
Singing mostly praise songs	49%	75%
Singing mostly contemporary Christian songs	47%	25%

What About Other Forms of Worship?

Although group singing is the primary worship form we use and that our kids like, there are other ways to worship that are making an impact on teens.

According to our kids, in addition to singing, the most commonly used forms of worship are: prayers of thanks (reported by 43% of teenagers); service projects (reported by 28% of teenagers); and Scripture readings (reported by 23% of teenagers). A few of the more adventuresome among us are also using silence (reported by 4% of teenagers) and liturgical dance (reported by 1% of teenagers).

> "ASK THE KIDS WHAT THEY WANT AND THEIR OPINIONS ON SONGS ... NOT THE SAME OLD THING EVERY WEEK!"
>
> —TENTH GRADER FROM NORTH CAROLINA

When you compare the overall rankings of what we use with what teenagers like most, we seem to be doing a fair job. Students rank their favorite worship forms in this order: 1) group singing; 2) service projects; 3) prayers of thanks; 4) Scripture readings and silence (tie); and 6) liturgical dance.

The only big areas of discrepancy, then, are that we seem to use prayers of thanks more than desired and service projects less than desired. Still, when you take into account that the majority of the kids took this survey while experiencing a service project, you could assume that influenced responses in this area.

What's interesting to note are the weightings in some of the lower categories. Only one in twenty-five respondents reported that silence was often used in worship, but more than double that number—roughly one in ten—rated silence as a form of worship they liked most. Likewise, about one in five of our teenagers experiences Scripture readings during worship time, but less than half of those (one in ten) chose that experience as the most meaningful.

Still, as a whole it's gratifying to discover that, for the most part, our group members like what we're providing as prompts for worship. In addition, significant portions of our teenagers are not only willing, but *like* to participate in a variety of worship forms—even something as rare as liturgical dance!

Worship Forms (Students could circle up to two.)

	Most-Used Worship Forms	Most-Desired Worship Forms
Group singing	57%	63%
Prayers of thanks	43%	25%
Service projects	28%	40%
Scripture readings	23%	9%
Silence	4%	9%
Liturgical dance	1%	7%

Chapter Summary and Observations

Now, let's take a few moments to recap what we've talked about and to consider a few implications.

Most teenagers are satisfied with the amount of time our youth groups regularly spend in worship, but a good portion of our kids (roughly one out of five) still longs for more.

> "Different types of people worship in different ways. Some people like that involvement, and some just like being by themselves."
>
> —Tenth-grade female from Indiana

These findings are encouraging. They tell us that our investment in youth group worship is paying dividends and meeting needs. The danger here is that we might read the numbers and then figure we can take it easy, relax a bit and concentrate on something else. That's simply not the case.

If we want to continue seeing our kids meet God in worship, we need to constantly reevaluate our time priorities to make sure we're not squeezing worship to make room for less important activities. Additionally, we need to remember that 20 percent of the students in our groups leave our worship table still hungry for more.

To meet the needs of those kids, consider scheduling "All Worship Meetings"—that is, meetings where the whole time is taken up with various worship activities—on a quarterly basis. Also, see if you can recruit some of these teenagers to help lead in group singing or some other worship activity. Finally, invest time and resources (including financial) to put together a first-rate worship band or to hire a first-rate worship leader. A skillful "conductor" of a worship experience adds immeasurably to the experience your teenagers receive.

> "I KNOW THAT ULTIMATELY WITH ALL MY MUSIC THE KIND OF UNDERLYING THEME IS KNOWING THAT IF CHRIST IS LIFTED UP HE WILL DRAW PEOPLE TO HIMSELF. I WANT THE MUSIC TO POINT PEOPLE TO HIM, THAT HE CAN DRAW THEM TO HIMSELF."
> —STEVEN CURTIS CHAPMAN[8]

The type of songs teenagers like to sing most are praise songs and contemporary Christian music hits.

It's time for us to face the music—literally! We can no longer allow ourselves (and our teenagers) to be held captive by our upbringing. We need to make a sincere effort to incorporate more contemporary Christian music into the group singing time at our youth groups.

Please don't misunderstand. I'm not advocating that we abandon praise songs. I'm simply suggesting that we lower the number of "old standards" we're singing and raise the number of newer songs we include.

Think about it. When we were teenagers "Jesus Music" (as CCM was widely called until the 1980s) was cutting-edge praise for us. We heard the tunes on the radio, and they moved us toward worshiping God. Then we came to church and got stuck with stuffy old hymns that were written mostly in a foreign language (King James-style English!).

Where would your worship experience be if your youth leaders, camp counselors, Campus Life and Youth for Christ leaders hadn't been willing to pick out some of the music you heard on the radio and adapt it for you? (Say good-bye to "Pharaoh, Pharaoh"!)

We have a responsibility to be those kinds of leaders for our kids and to incorporate the best of current CCM into everyday praise songs our group can sing when they gather together, or when kids are alone in their cars, in their quiet times or even in the shower.

Some quick suggestions for doing that:

> "I GREW UP IN A HOME WHERE PRAISE MUSIC WAS VERY MUCH A PART OF OUR LIVES. I ATTENDED MY FIRST CHRISTIAN CONCERT WHEN I WAS SIX WEEKS OLD. . . . I LOVE TO PRAISE GOD AND I LOVE HELPING OTHERS WORSHIP HIM."
> —REBECCA ST. JAMES[9]

- Listen to the radio, both mainstream and Christian. If you're handy with a guitar, see if you can make new, God-honoring lyrics to top 40 tunes. Keep an ear out for Christian songs with singable lyrics and hooky tunes. Then teach those to your kids.

- Utilize your local bookstore. You don't have to learn every new song by ear. A healthy majority of our favorite artists release songbooks to go along with their albums. Invest in these.

- Expose your kids to Christian music. Play the top CDs in *CCM Magazine*'s music charts for your kids before and after youth group. Look for songs to include as skit backgrounds or sermon illustrations.

- Ask kids what they like—and then sing them. Chances are your kids already are listening to Christian music. Find out which songs move them, then add those to your youth worship "playlist."

And, before we leave this topic, it's worth noting that although most of us have written off hymns, some of our teenagers haven't. It may be worthwhile to look for updated versions of classic hymns and then teach them to our teenagers. (Remember, most teenagers won't know these songs, which means they'll probably be open to trying these as "something new.")

A majority of teenagers rank group singing as their favorite form of worship, but large numbers of these kids are also open to participating in other worship forms as well.

This is exciting for several reasons. First, it means we're doing something right by including group singing in our youth meetings. Second, kids feel the impact of more than one worship form when they come to our groups, which reduces the possibility of perceived monotony. Third, it means our students have given us the freedom to try new, legitimate forms of worship.

So how do we respond? For starters, we need to remember not to underestimate our kids. For example, when was the last time you and your teenagers spent some worship time in silence following the advice of Psalm 46:10, which says, "Be still, and know that I am God. . . ." One of every ten kids in your group would love that— and if you tried it a few times, that number just might go up.

> "I THINK OUR BIGGEST [PURPOSE] IS TO EDIFY CHRISTIAN KIDS AND GET THEM PUMPED UP. . . . OUR AUDIENCES CAN EXPECT FUN, ENERGETIC STAGE SHOWS. WE TRY TO HAVE A JOYOUS TIME AS WE PRESENT THE MESSAGE OF CHRIST, A MESSAGE OF HOPE."
>
> —BOB HERDMAN, KEYBOARD AND GUITAR PLAYER, AUDIO ADRENALINE[10]

Second, we need to think about facilitating more service-oriented worship sessions. Romans 12:1 indicates that God honors this kind of worship, and a substantial number of our kids enjoy this as well. Perhaps we should take a cue from them and provide more opportunities to worship through serving.

Third, we need to examine and expand our own personal horizons in regard to worship forms. What stirs a spirit of praise within you? Does it happen on a hike through the mountains? at a contemporary Christian music concert? when you pause to catch a sunset? If so, why not invite a group of kids to join you in that activity?

Are you stuck in a rut personally in the forms of worship you utilize? Does worship for you mean only singing and maybe a service project or two? If so, look for new ways to worship God. Ask your students to help you brainstorm new ways to express praise to your Savior. Then try a few out in your personal devotions. If you find them to be meaningful, consider sharing them during youth group.

Two hundred and fifty years ago, George Handel powerfully experienced the presence of God in a moment of worship. Thankfully, God is still responsive to worship and is powerfully connecting with our kids in moments of praise today.

For Personal Reflection

Take a few moments now to process your own reaction to the information in this chapter. Use these questions to help spark your thinking:

- *How would you describe your own worship experience? Do you find that experience satisfying or not?*

- *In what ways does your personal experience in worship influence the worship time your youth group experiences?*

- *What have you discovered about your youth group's worship time through reading this chapter? Based on what you read, what new goals can you pursue to enhance that time?*

Chapter 3

WHAT I WISH MY YOUTH LEADER KNEW ABOUT . . .

CROWDBREAKERS AND GAMES

Why do these things always seem to happen to me? It was supposed to be a simple midweek meeting: Open with a crowd-breaker. Twenty minutes of games in the gym. Back into the youth room for more intense worship time and a speaker. Wrap up with prayer. Easy, right? Well, almost.

Everything went fine until game time. Crowding two hundred kids into the gymnasium, I'd planned for us to play a game affectionately called "Shoplifter." I formed four teams and had each team line up along a wall of the gym. Then, in the center of the room, I put a stash of great stuff—Frisbees, basketballs, footballs and a big tug-of-war rope. Teams would get points for each thing they were able to retrieve, and with a value of two hundred points, the rope was the big prize.

I started off easy, shouting "Everybody with green eyes, go!" Green-eyed kids scurried to the middle, snatched up all the equipment they could carry, then raced back to their cheering teams. So far, so good. Next came all kids wearing caps,

> INTERVIEWER: "IF YOU COULD CHANGE ONE THING ABOUT YOUR YOUTH GROUP'S CROWDBREAKERS AND GAMES, WHAT WOULD YOU CHANGE?"
> TENTH-GRADE MALE FROM A METHODIST CHURCH: "THE GAMES WOULD BE SMALLER. YOU BECOME CLOSER AND FIND OUT MORE ABOUT EACH OTHER'S PREFERENCES AND THINGS LIKE THAT."

anybody in red, youth leaders only, guys only, girls only and so on.

Finally, it was almost time to head back to the youth room, so for a last-minute contest, I shouted, "Everybody, go!" The ensuing melee was gobs-o-fun, especially the impromptu, four-way tug-of-war that quickly developed. And afterward group members started back to the room with a bounce in their steps.

That's when I realized how quickly a game can go awry. One of my volunteer leaders came rushing over to me. His name was Kevin, and he was a registered nurse.

"Mike," he said breathlessly, "one of the kids got hurt in that last round. She was reaching for a Frisbee when the tug-of-war started. Her arms got tangled in the rope, and I think she may have broken an arm!"

Broken an arm playing Shoplifter? Ridiculous! With all the authority of a youth leader who knows nothing of medicine, I declared, "There's no way she could've broken her arm. Put ice on it; she'll be fine." (Famous last words?)

Fifteen minutes later, Kevin was back again. "The ice isn't helping. I really do think she broke her arm. Shouldn't we take her to the hospital?"

Again, in my great wisdom, I patted Kevin on the shoulder. "Kevin, she probably just got a rope burn. But if you're really that concerned, call her parents and tell them what happened. See if they want to come pick her up."

Kevin ran off to my office to make the call, and I quickly forgot about the whole thing. The girl's parents showed up shortly and rushed their daughter to the hospital. It was there they discovered that Kevin was wrong. The girl didn't have one broken arm—she had two! The rope had trapped her arms together, and all the pressure of kids tugging in four different directions had fractured both her forearms.

And to make it worse, she was a first-time visitor who had come to youth group simply because a friend had invited her! Neither she nor her parents were even Christians.

Needless to say, I was ready to quit youth ministry and take up knitting once I found out I'd callously "prescribed" an ice pack for a kid who had broken both her arms playing a game I was leading. Thankfully, the parents (though unhappy with my performance) didn't sue, didn't go on the Jerry Springer show and didn't beat me up in a dark parking lot after church. They did, however, forbid their daughter from ever attending my group again.

> "MAKE IT FUN SO PEOPLE WANT TO COME."
>
> —TENTH GRADER FROM GEORGIA, GIVING ADVICE TO YOUTH PASTORS ABOUT HOW TO RUN A YOUTH MINISTRY.

Want to know something funny, though? That girl had had such a good time, up until she had broken her arms, that she actually argued with her parents about coming back. In spite of the physical injury, something about her experience with a crowdbreaker and a youth group game was appealing enough for her to risk coming back.

I never did see that girl again, but I've always remembered that playing a youth group game was enough to make her want to join our ministry. I hope she found someplace a little less dangerous to go!

Really Important?

After the arm-breaking incident, several friends asked me, "Is playing those games at youth group really all that important? Couldn't you just skip the crowdbreakers and games and focus on other things?"

I actually thought about it, briefly, but the next time I saw my kids charging pell-mell into a game of dodgeball, I knew I couldn't give up on these two standard elements of youth ministry. (I did take pains to be more careful, however!)

Based on the survey I did for this book, our students agree with that decision. In fact, more than nine of every ten students surveyed placed at least some importance on including crowdbreakers and games in a youth ministry. One in four said these activities aren't just important, they're *very* important.

"AS SILLY AS IT MAY SOUND, THE AMOUNT OF POINTS YOU GIVE CAN ACTUALLY INCREASE THE ENJOYMENT AND EXCITEMENT OF THOSE WHO ARE PLAYING. POINTS ARE FREE, SO YOU DON'T HAVE TO BE STINGY WITH THEM. GIVE LOTS OF POINTS— A THOUSAND POINTS! THREE THOU- SAND POINTS! AFTER ALL, WHO WANTS TO PLAY A GAME FOR FIFTY MEASLY POINTS WHEN HE CAN WIN THREE THOUSAND POINTS? LIVE A LITTLE—GIVE TEN THOUSAND POINTS!"

—WAYNE RICE AND MIKE YACONELLI[2]

When you look at how those numbers break down across regions, it reveals an interesting trend. A healthy number of kids—27 percent, to be exact—from eastern and midwestern regions say that crowdbreakers and games are very important. Likewise, a similar number (26%) of teenagers from the southwest and western U.S. rate these activities highly. When you move to the central and southern U.S., however, the number of kids very interested in crowdbreakers and games jumps by about one-third to 36 percent!

The implications here are hard to pin down. Does this mean that youth leaders in the central and southern states have better games? That kids on the coasts are "too sophisticated" to really let loose and enjoy a good game? I'm not sure, but I do know one thing. If I were a youth pastor from the central or southern part of our nation, I'd want to give careful attention to games and crowdbreakers in my ministry. If I didn't, I'd be potentially ignoring more than one-third of the kids in my youth group.

The other significant statistical difference shows up in the gender breakdown. Surprisingly, girls are more likely to value a good game or crowdbreaker than guys. What makes this surprising is that teenage girls are generally considered to be too prissy, unwilling to risk messing up their hair or makeup, likely to regard an activity as "childish" or uncool, to play many games. Fortunately, that's just not true. To paraphrase an old movie, "If you play it, they will come!"

When you examine the data according to age, it seems the smallest group of those surveyed—the seventh graders—are least likely to rate crowdbreakers and games highly. Still, a healthy one in five are looking forward to some kind of fun activity each week. The other grades are pretty comparable in their interest, with anywhere from 26 percent to 31 percent of eighth through twelfth graders rating crowdbreakers and games as "very important." Of this group, sophomore and juniors in high school are most enthusiastic about these kinds of activities.

"HOW IMPORTANT TO YOU ARE CROWDBREAKERS AND GAMES IN A YOUTH GROUP?"

Very important	29%
Moderately important	42%
Slightly important	22%
Not important at all	8%

PERCENTAGE OF YOUTH GROUP MEMBERS WHO SAY THAT CROWDBREAKERS AND GAMES IN A YOUTH MINISTRY ARE "VERY IMPORTANT" TO THEM, LISTED BY CATEGORIES

BY GENDER:

Males	24%
Females	31%

BY REGION:

Eastern and Midwestern Regions	27%
Central and Southern Regions	36%
Southwestern and Western Regions	26%

BY GRADE:

7th Grade	20%
8th Grade	30%
9th Grade	27%
10th Grade	31%
11th Grade	30%
12th Grade	26%

Name That Word

It's nice to hear that a strong majority of our teenagers enjoy participating in crowdbreakers and games because we play a lot of them over the course of a normal ministry year. So, how are we doing in this area? We know kids like games, but do they like *our* games?

Students were given a list of adjectives that could describe a crowdbreaker or game. Included on the list were positive words such as "fun" and "creative," as well as negative terms such as "boring" and "childish" and (hopefully) neutral terms such as "competitive" and "cooperative." Youth group members were asked to choose two of these words to describe the crowdbreakers and games they experience at their home churches.

Students overwhelmingly described their games and crowdbreakers using emotion-laden words, with very few (about one out of every thirteen kids) choosing a neutral term. The two words most often chosen to describe games and crowdbreakers were positive ones: "fun" (57%) and "creative" (35%). The two words students chose least often to describe our fun-time activities were both positive ("affirming," 2%) and negative ("complicated," 2%).

For starters, that tells us that kids have noticed we're interested in having fun too and that we're trying to be creative in the ways we have fun in youth group. Additionally, we're not sacrificing "do-ability" for our creativity, being careful to plan activities that are easily understood by our teens. (OK, go ahead and pat yourself on the back!)

Now the bad news. It's a travesty that so few of our teenagers find our crowdbreakers and games affirming. Although 21 percent describe these activities as "relationship-building," they're apparently not being encouraged much by them. It seems that alarmingly few teammates are affirming each other during games, few leaders are recognizing individual contributions and little (or no) activity is geared toward building up kids in the group.

This is particularly disheartening considering the fact that crowdbreakers were included in this portion of the survey. Crowdbreakers, by their nature, should get kids talking to each other and learning about each other. This, then, ought to be a natural opportunity for kids to affirm each other as well—but it's not. We can, and should, do better in this area.

> "YOUTH GROUP GAMES ARE LIKE FOLK SONGS—THEY CHANGE AS THEY MOVE FROM GROUP TO GROUP. SOMEONE ADDS A TWIST HERE OR MODIFIES A RULE THERE, AND THE GAME CHANGES AS IT PASSES THROUGH DIFFERENT GROUPS' HANDS. AND THAT'S EXACTLY AS IT SHOULD BE."
>
> —MIKAL KEEFER[3]

Another word that showed up strongly on the survey was "childish," with roughly one in five kids describing their group's games and crowdbreakers this way. If there was a complaint about our crowdbreakers and games, the hard-to-define "childish factor" was it.

INTERVIEWER: "IF YOU COULD CHANGE ONE THING ABOUT YOUR YOUTH GROUP'S CROWDBREAKERS AND GAMES, WHAT WOULD YOU CHANGE?"
NINTH-GRADE FEMALE FROM A REFORMED CHURCH: "NOTHING REALLY. THEY'RE REALLY FUN!"

Caught between childhood and adulthood, our teenagers are very sensitive to being thought of as "little kids." We would do well, then, to plan games that treat our participants more like adults than children.

Happily, very few teenagers described our crowdbreakers and games with those dreaded words, "boring" and "embarrassing." Ten to fifteen years ago (back in the days of whipped cream pranks and water-filled pants), I'd wager both these terms would've shown up more than the seven percent each took in this time. We've come a long way, baby!

POSITIVE, NEGATIVE OR NEUTRAL?

57% of students used at least one positive term to describe their youth group's crowdbreakers and games.

18% of students used at least one negative term to describe their youth group's crowdbreakers and games.

8% of students used at least one neutral term to describe their youth group's crowdbreakers and games.

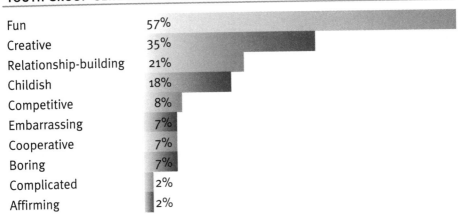

"WHICH WORDS BEST DESCRIBE THE CROWDBREAKERS AND GAMES YOUR YOUTH GROUP GENERALLY USES?"

Fun	57%
Creative	35%
Relationship-building	21%
Childish	18%
Competitive	8%
Embarrassing	7%
Cooperative	7%
Boring	7%
Complicated	2%
Affirming	2%

What Games Do Teens Like?

Now, let's talk a little specifically about games. We know our kids like to play games, but what kinds of games do they like? To find out, I identified nine broad categories of games and presented those to the survey takers. Although these nine categories certainly don't encompass all games, they do cover a majority of the game styles we use in ministry.

> "EVER SINCE CHURCHES AND PARA-CHURCH GROUPS HAVE BEGUN TRYING TO REACH URBAN TEENAGERS, RECREATION AND ATHLETICS HAVE BEEN MAJOR OUTREACH TOOLS. . . . THIS APPROACH IS GENERALLY SUCCESSFUL."
>
> —EUGENE C. ROEHLKEPARTAIN[4]

Teenagers were allowed to choose up to two game styles they liked best. Surprisingly, even with the two-vote possibilities, no one style of game garnered a majority of teen approval. The closest any category came to a majority was 47 percent, pulled in by the general category "team competitions."

That suggests two things. First, on the "bad news" side, we still haven't found that category of games that *everybody* (or nearly everybody) loves. That means that on any given day we lead a game at youth group, potentially more than half the kids involved don't really give a hoot about our chosen game. Second, on the "good news" side, this suggests a majority of our teenagers aren't locked into one game style and are therefore open to playing a variety of games at youth group meetings.

> "GOD ENJOYS PLAY."
>
> —DR. CALVIN SEERVELD[5]

Team competitions are far and away the most appealing game style among teenagers. In fact, team competitions received nearly half of all kids' votes, settling it firmly in the number one spot. Meanwhile, the opposite game style, individual competitions, ranked dead last, with only one of every twenty-five students choosing that option.

Notice, however, that although relays would count as a team competition, surprisingly few teenagers are interested in that game style. One impassioned young person even wrote on the survey that, when it came to game styles, he liked "everything except relays!" In truth, 93 percent of our kids—more than nine out of ten—agreed with him, omitting this youth group staple from their choices at all. Perhaps we'd be wise to do the same.

Physical/active games rated second in the overall survey results. As one eighth grader commented, "I love physical games such as Tag! Some games we just stand around, and it would be more fun if our group did more physical games. I especially like Elbow Tag. It gets everybody talking and stuff."

There are probably a plethora of reasons why kids like physical games, but a few spring quickly to mind. Physical games where kids are up and moving around create an opportunity to release pent-up energy in a safe and controlled setting—something that's good for kids and leaders both. Physical games also generally require teamwork, which contributes to relationship-building within the group. Because GenX and Millennial teenagers typically value relationships, games that contribute relationally increase in perceived value as well.

An interesting trend emerges, however, when you look at how group members in each grade ranked physical/active games. It seems seventh graders start off with a strong interest in these kinds of games, then their interest wanes in eighth grade. The downward spiral continues until it reaches a low ebb during tenth grade. Starting in eleventh grade, interest in physical/active games takes a jump back up, and by twelfth grade they are again the number one interest among respondents.

I think it's no surprise that the decline in interest toward physical/active games happens during eighth through tenth grade. This is also the time when puberty wreaks the most havoc on kids, making them self-conscious about their physical performance.

> "WE PLAYED [THE 'BIGGER AND BETTER'] GAME AT MY DAUGHTER'S BIRTHDAY PARTY. THE BOYS' TEAM CAME BACK WITH AN OLD SOFA, A TOILET, AND AN UMBRELLA. THE GIRLS HAD A SKATEBOARD RAMP—WHICH SAT IN FRONT OF MY HOUSE FOR A WEEK."
> —JIM BURNS[6]

Students just beginning to experience puberty (seventh graders) or on the tail end of this life experience (twelfth graders) have much less concern about their physical image, so they are able to enjoy these kinds of games more. (Among twelfth graders, it probably doesn't hurt, either, that they're typically the biggest and most experienced group members and as such can sometimes feel they have an advantage over the other grades—which makes any game more enjoyable!)

With the strong showing of team competitions and physical/active games, the ranking "sports-related games" received (number three) could be expected. After all, games such as football, volleyball, broomhockey and the like combine the best of both the first two categories: teamwork and activity.

The other category worth noting is that of mental games. Nearly one in five of the kids in your youth group enjoys these kinds of competitions immensely. I imagine that when mental games are also part of team competitions, that number would go even higher. So be careful when you assume your group members don't want to think during a game—many of them do.

The last item worth bringing out concerns elimination games. To put it bluntly, they stink. Again, more than nine out of ten teenagers refused to choose this category, though it appears often in a youth ministry context. Why? Think about it. Only one person really enjoys a game like Musical Chairs—the winner. The rest must spend some or all of the game sitting on the sidelines watching other kids have fun. My advice? Eliminate the elimination games and your students will have a lot more fun.

"WHICH GAME STYLES DO YOU LIKE BEST?"

Team competitions	47%
Physical/active games	29%
Sports-related games	25%
Mental games	18%
Noncompetitive games	15%
Elimination games	7%
Relays	7%
Word games	7%
Individual competitions	4%

WHERE TEENAGERS RANKED PHYSICAL/ACTIVE GAMES AMONG THEIR FAVORITE GAMES STYLES, BY GRADES AND PERCENTAGES:

GRADE	PERCENTAGE	WHERE RANKED
7th Grade	40%	1 (tie with team competitions)
8th Grade	33%	2
9th Grade	24%	3
10th Grade	21%	3
11th Grade	25%	3
12th Grade	42%	1 (tie with team competitions)

Chapter Summary and Observations

A large majority of teenagers report that crowdbreakers and games in a youth group are important to them. In short: Kids just wanna have fun.

Certainly crowdbreakers and games aren't the only reason that teenagers flock to your youth group, but it definitely is one of the reasons. Because of that, a youth group with a healthy complement of crowdbreakers and games is more likely to draw teenagers than one that doesn't have them.

> "RELATIONSHIPS ARE OFTEN BUILT THROUGH GAMES. GAMES ARE A COMMON ACTIVITY THAT'S LESS THREATENING THAN SHARING PRAYER REQUESTS. WATCH HOW KIDS BUILD RELATIONSHIPS—IT'S USUALLY THROUGH SHARED ACTIVITIES. SO USE GAMES AS A PART OF YOUR MINISTRY OF BUILDING RELATIONSHIPS WITHIN YOUR GROUP."
>
> —TIGER MCLUEN[7]

Unfortunately, many kids who come to our churches never get to play games in youth group. I was surprised at the number of survey respondents who, in answering questions about group crowdbreakers and games, wrote in statements such as "We don't do them" or "We never do any" or "We don't play games."

These kids—though a minority—weren't from one or two isolated groups. Geographically and denominationally, they were all over the map—from Pennsylvania to Minnesota to Texas to Colorado, and from Catholic churches to Presbyterian churches to Christian churches and more.

During a follow-up phone interview, we asked one tenth grader from Indiana what she'd change about her group's crowdbreakers and games. She responded emphatically, "I'd have some! We don't have any." If yours is one of those groups that has eliminated crowdbreakers or games from your meetings, my suggestion would be simple. Follow the advice of this girl from Indiana and "have some."

For the most part, students see their crowdbreakers and games as "fun" and "creative." However, a significant number feel their group's activities in this area are "childish," and nearly no one feels affirmed during these activities.

Judging by our teenagers' assessment of our performance in this area, we're doing well. So keep up the good work! Remember, these activities are supposed to be fun—so do your best to make them that way. Borrow the creativity of others to find games for your group by investing in a library of games books (a large number of which are available at your local Christian bookstore).

We do need to be careful, though, not to use crowdbreakers or games that could be perceived as childish. Typically, anything that could be associated with elementary school is off-limits.

No one style of game is able to appeal strongly to a majority of teenagers, but healthy numbers of teens are likely to enjoy team competitions, physical or active games and sports-related games. Elimination games and relays are generally unpopular among youth group members.

The obvious application of this data is simply to vary the kinds of crowdbreakers and games you use. You're not always going to please everybody every time. But you can please everybody at one time or another by using a variety of game styles regularly in your ministry. Also, pay special attention to those games that require team competition and/or physical activity, as these are the styles that will appeal most often to your kids.

The second application is for us to face up to the fact that most teenagers don't like elimination games or relays. Unfortunately, these are the kinds of games I've witnessed *often* at youth groups from

Connecticut to California. Based on the survey results, I'd suggest that these are game styles best suited to a bygone era—and as such we should bid them good-bye for now. Who knows, ten to fifteen years in the future, they may come back in vogue.

For Personal Reflection

Take a few moments now to process your own reaction to the information in this chapter. Use these questions to help spark your thinking:

- *What expectations did you have as you started this chapter? How did the survey results confirm or challenge those expectations?*

- *How do your crowdbreakers and games compare to what teenagers say they like best? Is there room for improvement? If so, how? If not, what are you doing well?*

- *What are five reasons you can think of to explain why 93 percent of teenagers attach at least some importance to crowdbreakers and games in your ministry? What does that say to you as their leader?*

> "THEY DEVOTED THEMSELVES
> TO THE APOSTLES' TEACHING
> AND TO THE FELLOWSHIP,
> TO THE BREAKING OF BREAD
> AND TO PRAYER."
> —ACTS 2:42

Chapter 4

WHAT I WISH MY YOUTH LEADER KNEW ABOUT . . .

SUNDAY SCHOOL

In 1994, Chuck Colson (founder of Prison Fellowship) was honored to visit England's Buckingham Palace. While there, he had an audience with Prince Philip.

Since the prince knew of Colson's ongoing ministry to prisoners around the world, he engaged Colson in a conversation on the topic of Britain's increasing crime rate. Turning to Chuck, the prince asked, "What can we do about crime here in England?"

Rather than suggesting expected things such as increased police staff, widespread curfews, bigger law enforcement budgets or "zero-tolerance" attitudes, Colson proposed something even more radical.

> "LEADERS ARE TEACHERS. NO MATTER WHAT THE ENTERPRISE—A FAMILY, SCHOOL, CHURCH, OR BUSINESS—LEADERS ARE TEACHERS. THE TERMS ARE NOT INTERCHANGEABLE; NOT ALL TEACHERS ARE LEADERS, BUT ALL LEADERS *ARE* TEACHERS."
>
> —BOB BRINER AND RAY PRITCHARD[1]

"Send more children to Sunday school," he declared.

The prince chuckled, sure that Chuck was joking—but he wasn't, and here's why. According to a study by sociologist Christie Davies, British society in the early 1800s was subjected to high levels of crime and violence. According to Davies' study, that high crime rate plummeted in the later 1800s and early 1900s, resulting in a safer British society as a whole.

During that same time period, Sunday school classes proliferated in Britain. In fact, by 1888, three-fourths of all English children—75 percent—were enrolled in Sunday school.

ACCORDING TO STANDARD PUBLISHING AND THE BARNA RESEARCH GROUP, 93 PERCENT OF AMERICA'S CHURCHES HAVE A SUNDAY SCHOOL PROGRAM IN PLACE FOR JUNIOR HIGH/MIDDLE SCHOOL STUDENTS. EIGHTY-SIX PERCENT HAVE SUNDAY SCHOOL FOR SENIOR HIGHERS.[3]

Is it merely coincidence that high levels of involvement in Sunday school corresponded with lower crime rates? Colson doesn't think so—and more recent history seems to prove him right. Commenting on current situations, Chuck says, "Attendance has fallen off to one-third its peak level, with a corresponding increase in crime and disorder."[2]

In short, Chuck Colson views Sunday school as vitally important—and, since a recent poll by the Barna Research Group revealed that nine of ten churches in America have a Sunday school program,[4] your church leaders probably think Sunday school is important too. But how about your teenagers? What are their views of Sunday school? Let's find out.

Mixed Reviews

Of all the topics covered in this survey, this was the one that elicited the strongest—and most divergent—views from teenagers. For the most part, Sunday school is not a neutral issue among our kids. In a follow-up phone interview with one of the survey respondents, one teen said, "They [teenagers] go because their parents make them go.

"The youth pastor should make it youth-oriented, not necessarily go by a set curriculum."

Consider some other comments shared in follow-up conversations:

"They [teenagers] don't feel comfortable and can't speak their minds [at Sunday school]. The youth pastor should make them feel more comfortable."—Twelfth-grade female from Illinois

"I've never really had a negative experience [at Sunday school]. . . . My youth pastor makes it really fun—but he's leaving soon to finish his studies."—Tenth-grade male from Texas

> FROM A CARTOON BY
> RON WHEELER:
> A GRIM-FACED TEACHER
> BRANDISHING A POINTER STANDS
> IN FRONT OF AN EMPTY
> CLASSROOM AND SAYS:
> "WHAT'S THIS RUMOR I HEAR
> ABOUT SOME OF YOU SKIPPING MY
> SUNDAY SCHOOL CLASS?"[5]

"Most of the time, it's stuff we've been hearing for years like 'sex' and 'drugs.' We know it's wrong and don't want to hear more lectures. Ask the youth group what they'd like to study and discuss in Sunday school."—Tenth grader from a nondenominational church

"They [teenagers] think it's going to be boring, [but] my youth pastor makes things related to today, things to make the Bible easier to understand."—Eleventh grader from a charismatic church

"I think they [teenagers] don't want to be [at Sunday school]. They'd rather go home than stay at church and learn about God. The pastor should make it more fun. Some are boring, like Bible games."—Ninth grader from a Reformed church in Indiana

Unfortunately, this ninth grader from the Hoosier state isn't the only student to complain that Sunday school is boring. In fact, when I asked students to tell me what words best described their Sunday school experience, one in four kids chose "boring"—landing that word in a tie for the most-chosen word.

There's more. Although about the same percentage of girls (24%) chose the word "boring" to describe Sunday school, the girls in this survey ranked that word as their number one choice outright. The same is true for teenagers living in the central and southern regions of the country, as well as kids in the ninth and tenth grades. With 29 percent (nearly one in three students) choosing this word, ninth graders rate as the most bored segment of our Sunday schools.

> "CHRISTIAN EDUCATION MATTERS MUCH MORE THAN WE EXPECTED. . . . INVOLVEMENT IN AN EFFECTIVE CHRISTIAN EDUCATION PROGRAM HAS THE STRONGEST TIE TO A PERSON'S GROWTH IN FAITH. WHILE OTHER CONGREGATIONAL FACTORS ALSO MATTER, NOTHING MATTERS MORE THAN EFFECTIVE CHRISTIAN EDUCATION. AND THIS IS AS TRUE FOR ADULTS AS IT IS FOR ADOLESCENTS."
>
> —PETER BENSON AND CAROLYN ELKIN[6]

Surprisingly, when I asked my panel of youth leaders to identify the words they thought teenagers would use to describe Sunday school, they too rated "boring" high. It came in second on their list. The word they chose as number one was "passive"—which honestly isn't much better than "boring."

What does this mean? Well, I hate to be the one to admit this, but the truth is that Sunday school bores our kids—they know it, and we know it.

Statistical Schizophrenia

So what do you think? Should we chuck Sunday school out the window and try something else? Not necessarily, at least not yet. As I mentioned earlier, Sunday school was the one topic on the survey that seemed to elicit the broadest spectrum of opinion from teenagers.

Remember how I said that enough kids chose "boring" to describe their Sunday school experience that it finished in first place as the word most chosen? Well, an exactly equal percentage of teenagers described their Sunday school experience as "thought-provoking"— something that would generally be regarded as a positive evaluation of Sunday school. So, it seems that equal numbers of kids view Sunday school as really bad or really good.

> "TIME SPENT IN PRAYER IS
> NEVER WASTED."
> —FRANCIS FENELON[7]

This type of statistical schizophrenia showed up all through this portion of the survey! Consider:

Nineteen percent of teenagers (roughly one in five) described their Sunday school experience as "valuable," while 19 percent of teenagers (again, nearly one in five) described Sunday school as "simple."

Roughly one out of every eight students (12%) finds Sunday school to be "exciting" and "deep." And the same number of students (12%) feels Sunday school is hopelessly "out-of-touch."

Nine percent of our teenagers consider Sunday school a "time-waster," and 7 percent regard it as "passive," but another 6 percent say it's a challenging experience. Of the top eight words chosen by teenagers in this category, five were positive terms and three were negative terms. The implication here, then, is that your youth group's Sunday school program has the *potential* to impact a good number of teenagers for Christ, but is falling short for some kids.

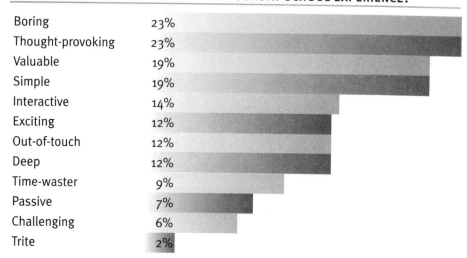

"WHICH WORDS BEST DESCRIBE YOUR SUNDAY SCHOOL EXPERIENCE?"

Boring	23%
Thought-provoking	23%
Valuable	19%
Simple	19%
Interactive	14%
Exciting	12%
Out-of-touch	12%
Deep	12%
Time-waster	9%
Passive	7%
Challenging	6%
Trite	2%

Whatever Happened to Prayer?

To discover where we may be falling short, it's important to look at what we actually do during Sunday school. Our top three activities, according to teenagers, are: 1) discussion; 2) hearing a speaker; and 3) worksheets.

Curious what the three activities we engage in *least* often are? Bible reading, learning activities and prayer. What in the world are we *doing*?

Let's examine this a bit. More than half of our teenagers say we allot a significant amount of time for discussion. I find this news to be encouraging—especially when you consider that kids earlier said they learn the most from a youth talk when it involves opportunity for discussion (see chapter 1).

Pardon my directness (and remember, I'm speaking to myself as well), but the rest of these results are a travesty. We've heard for years the statistics about learning: Spoken or written communication yields only a 5 to 10 percent retention rate. Direct experience, on the other hand, yields an 80 to 90 percent retention rate.[8]

If we know these things, why have we dedicated so much time to methods that are ineffective (lecture and worksheets) and so little time to methods that increase learning (learning activities) and in activities that direct kids into experiencing God personally (Bible reading and prayer)? When we spend more time in Sunday school doing "worksheets" than we spend in the Bible and in prayer, we're making some very poor investments with our resources.

Earlier in this chapter we explored the words teenagers used to describe Sunday school and wondered why there were so many different perceptions—and why a significant number of those perceptions were negative. I believe the answer is in this statistic: Out of the 403 teenagers who took this survey, only five students (no, that's not a misprint) reported that prayer was given the *majority* of time in their Sunday school classes. That's just barely 1 percent of all surveyed. (That is not to say that we are not spending *some* time in prayer, but it is not the priority.) For some reason we've decided there's more value in having our kids dive into worksheets and the like than in having our kids immerse themselves in prayer.

Compare that number with these facts on prayer two colleagues and I documented in another work:[9]

- Sixty-three percent of teenagers say they pray every week.

- Sixty-two percent of teenagers and young adults believe that "God hears all people's prayers and has the power to answer those prayers."

- More than half of Christian teenagers (55%) say they "pray for God's help for others."

- Just less than half of all American teenagers (42%) report that they "pray alone frequently."

- Among churchgoing teenagers, 40 percent say they are interested or very interested in "learning how to pray."

Prayer is supposed to be a vital part of any Christian's life, and teenagers are plainly interested in praying. How can we expect our teenagers to grow more intimate with God if we won't schedule significant time for them to meet with God through prayer?

E. M. BOUNDS ONCE SAID, "THE MORE PRAYING THERE IS IN THE WORLD, THE BETTER THE WORLD WILL BE, THE MIGHTIER THE FORCES AGAINST EVIL EVERYWHERE. . . . PRAYER IS NO FITFUL SHORT-LIVED THING. IT IS NO VOICE CRYING UNHEARD AND UNHEEDED IN THE SILENCE. IT IS A VOICE WHICH GOES INTO GOD'S EAR, AND IT LIVES AS LONG AS GOD'S EAR IS OPEN TO HOLY PLEAS, AS LONG AS GOD'S HEART IS ALIVE TO HOLY THINGS. GOD SHAPES THE WORLD BY PRAYER."[10]

The theme Scripture for this chapter is Acts 2:42, which describes the activities of the early church. Listen again to what that verse says: "They devoted themselves to the apostles' teaching and to the fellowship, to the breaking of bread and *to prayer*." (Italics mine.)

If we want God to shape our Sunday schools and our teenagers, we need to be diligent to schedule more time in that Sunday school for prayer. As it is now, prayer seems to be a low priority during the Sunday school hour, and I believe we're paying the price for that in our youth groups as a whole.

And I'd be remiss if I didn't call us to task for one other grave failing in the area of Sunday school. With only 6 percent of our teenagers reporting a significant time in Bible reading during Sunday school, we've denied them opportunity to get to know the Bible for themselves as well. At the risk of sounding like an old Baptist or Pentecostal preacher, I must say that we need to repent—and we need to do it now.

OK, enough sermonizing. I'll move on.

"WHAT DOES YOUR GROUP SPEND THE MOST TIME ON DURING SUNDAY SCHOOL?"

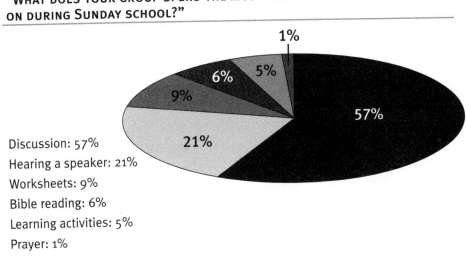

Discussion: 57%
Hearing a speaker: 21%
Worksheets: 9%
Bible reading: 6%
Learning activities: 5%
Prayer: 1%

A Few Last Findings About Sunday School

Based on what I had discovered so far, I expected teenagers to feel uncomfortable about bringing their friends to class. That's also what my survey of youth leaders indicated, with about two-thirds of these ministry veterans suggesting that teenagers would be uncomfortable inviting a friend to join the class.

Thankfully, our perceptions in this area are wrong. Although we may fail in other areas, at least (for the most part) we haven't failed in making our Sunday school classes a place where kids feel welcome. In truth, just over one in four teenagers (28%) feels uncomfortable asking a friend to tag along. By contrast, more than seven of every ten teenagers (71%) have no qualms about inviting a friend to Sunday school. Additionally, more than one-third of our kids say they feel "very comfortable" doing this.

Those group members who are likely to feel the least comfortable are eighth graders, with 42 percent admitting to some level of discomfort

"STOP AND THINK ABOUT HOW YOU'D EDUCATE SOMEONE WHO'D COME TO WORK FOR YOU. CONSIDER A NEWLY-HIRED SECRETARY. YOU WOULDN'T ATTEMPT TO TRAIN YOUR NEW SECRETARY WITH A PILE OF CROSSWORDS, FILL-IN-THE-BLANKS, AND HIDDEN-WORD PUZZLES. YOU WOULDN'T SCRAMBLE THE WORD MACINTOSH TO TEACH YOUR SECRETARY HOW TO USE THE COMPUTER. YOU WOULDN'T INSIST YOUR NEW SECRETARY PORE OVER THE COPY MACHINE'S USERS MANUAL TO FIND SOME WORTHLESS FACT LIKE THE DATE IT WAS INVENTED. YOU WOULDN'T REQUIRE YOUR SECRETARY TO SPEND VALUABLE TIME MEMORIZING EVERY CHURCH MEMBER'S ADDRESS AND TELEPHONE NUMBER.

"NO, YOU KNOW INTUITIVELY THESE SILLY METHODS WILL NOT HELP YOUR SECRETARY QUICKLY AND EFFECTIVELY LEARN THE JOB. COMMON SENSE TELLS YOU THERE'S A BETTER WAY TO EDUCATE YOUR SECRETARY.

"IT'S TIME ALSO TO APPLY SOME COMMON SENSE TO ALL LEARNING IN THE CHURCH."

—THOM & JOANI SCHULTZ[11]

at the thought of inviting a friend to Sunday school. Ninth graders, by contrast, are the most comfortable, with 40 percent saying they feel "very comfortable" inviting a friend.

Unfortunately, when we check our effectiveness in Sunday school, we don't rate as well. I asked teenagers how helpful Sunday school was in their spiritual growth, and 30% said it was "often helpful." Thirteen percent (or one in eight students) report that Sunday school is "not much help" at all when it comes to growing spiritually.

That means, if we're teaching a class of ten students, only three of those teenagers are being helped spiritually on any given week. One to two of those kids get absolutely nothing. And for the rest we have a hit-or-miss ministry. Some weeks they're helped, other weeks they're not.

Imagine if your local grocery store operated this way. What kind of response would you have if that store aired a commercial with a pitch man enthusiastically saying, "For every one thousand shoppers, we guarantee three hundred of you will get food! Of course, 130 of you won't get anything, no matter how often you come to our store. And for the other 570 of you, sometimes we'll let you get food, other times you'll get nothing! So come on over to our place and shop today!"

After seeing that commercial, how often would you want to shop at that store? How often will your teenagers come back if your Sunday school is perceived the same way? It seems this is at least one more area in which we can improve.

"HOW COMFORTABLE DO YOU FEEL ABOUT INVITING YOUR FRIENDS TO JOIN YOU IN SUNDAY SCHOOL?"

	TEEN RESPONSES	YOUTH LEADER EXPECTATIONS
Very comfortable	36%	10%
Moderately comfortable	35%	25%
Slightly uncomfortable	15%	40%
Not comfortable at all	13%	25%

SUNDAY SCHOOL'S EFFECTIVENESS, ACCORDING TO TEENAGERS

"Occasionally/sometimes helpful in my spiritual growth"	57%
"Often helpful in my spiritual growth"	30%
"Not much help in my spiritual growth"	13%

Chapter Summary and Observations

Sunday school can be boring—teens know it and we know it. At the same time, a good percentage of teenagers have positive feelings toward the Sunday school experience.

"I DISCOVERED THAT THE ELEVEN O'CLOCK HOUR ON SUNDAY MORNING WAS ODDLY UNLIKE ANY OTHER HOUR IN THE WEEK. AT NO OTHER TIME DID I SIT FOR THIRTY OR FORTY MINUTES IN A STRAIGHT-BACKED CHAIR AND LISTEN TO SOMEONE LECTURE ME. . . . I IDENTIFIED WITH ONE OF FLANNERY O'CONNER'S IN-LAWS, WHO STARTED ATTENDING CHURCH BECAUSE THE SERVICE WAS 'SO HORRIBLE, HE KNEW THERE MUST BE SOMETHING ELSE THERE TO MAKE THE PEOPLE COME.'"

—PHILIP YANCEY[13]

In spite of the fact that a good number of our students find Sunday school to be "boring" or worse, they haven't given up on us yet. That means we don't have to give up either—but we do need to consider making a change.

Regarding the state of the church today, Dr. George Barna eloquently states, "As difficult as it may be to . . . think about changing—radically, in some cases—the alternative is worse: to continue doing what we have been doing, the way we have been doing it, and being an accessory to the moral and spiritual disintegration of America."[12] I believe those words apply to our youth Sunday school programs as well.

So what kinds of changes should we make? Here's what our teenagers suggest:

"Make it more kid-oriented. Let them take over and [lead] the youth group. Basically, hand over the leadership part to us so we can do it."

"Ask kids what *they* want to do."

"Make stuff more interesting and more funner [*sic*]. Ask the kids if they like the lesson, what they learned, and if they understood what he said."

"Make it interesting and pertaining to recent events and things kids care about—not things they can't relate to."

"Let teenagers experience things themselves!"

"The most important thing is to let the youth get involved."

And to all these things I'd add one more: Let us pray.

We've been negligent in making prayer a priority in Sunday school.

If we tell our kids they should pray, and then neglect to devote significant time to praying in Sunday school, we're actually communicating the opposite of what we preach. We're saying that prayer is a meaningless activity, a trite formality that holds no real power or connection with God. If we truly believed that, I doubt many of us would be in youth ministry at all.

I would suggest we do three things to remedy this situation. First, we need to change our perception of prayer. It's not a time-filler. It's not an obligatory opener and standard wrap-up. It's not something we cut if we're running short on time or expand if we're running long.

Prayer, rather, is a unique, miraculous opportunity for each person in your youth group (you included) to intimately approach the Father who both made us and loves us. To treat it otherwise is to miss the true value of this precious gift.

> "NOT MANY SERMONS LIFT UP THE EXAMPLES OF MARTYRED SEVENTH-GRADE SUNDAY-SCHOOL TEACHERS."
>
> —DOUG HALL[14]

Second, we need to let our actions reflect God's priorities. God believes in prayer, and we *claim* to believe in it. Therefore, we should let our actions in Sunday school reflect that. We need to be purposeful about planning time for prayer. We need to be inflexible about letting other less-important activities crowd out that time. We need to be diligent about teaching our students how to pray and then letting them practice it regularly. If we would act out what we say we believe concerning prayer, I guarantee it would revolutionize the Sunday school experience of our teenagers and ourselves.

Finally, we need to repent—publicly—and ask our kids to join us in a renewed commitment to prayer. I think it would be appropriate to apologize publicly to our teenagers and to God for failing to make prayer a priority in Sunday school. That kind of public honesty models for kids the power of repentance as well as the effect of forgiveness, and helps both them and us be accountable to practice prayer on a more regular, purposeful basis.

> "IF WE FILL THE SUNDAY SCHOOLS, WE CAN CHANGE HEARTS AND RESTORE SOCIETY."
> —CHARLES W. COLSON[15]

Teenagers generally feel comfortable in our Sunday school classes, but our classes are often ineffective in helping kids grow spiritually.

It's great that a majority of teenagers generally have no real apprehension about inviting friends to Sunday school. It's not so great that our classes don't offer much in the way of regular, helpful instruction for spiritual growth.

I'd recommend using Sunday school to teach—and let kids practice—more of the spiritual disciplines such as how to pray, how to study the Bible, when and how to fast, how to use silence, how to meditate on Scripture and so on. By reinforcing the habits of a healthy spiritual life in this way, we help students assume responsibility for their own progress in faith and increase the potential of making Sunday school a place that really and truly helps kids grow spiritually week in and week out.

For Personal Reflection

Take a few moments now to process your own reaction to the information in this chapter. Use these questions to help spark your thinking:

- *If you were to estimate the percentage of kids in your group who are bored with Sunday school, what number would you use? Why do you suppose those kids are feeling that way?*

- *What keeps you from devoting more time to prayer in your group's Sunday school class? What can you do about that?*

- *What changes can you make in the next four weeks to help make your Sunday school a place that consistently helps teenagers grow spiritually? What obstacles do you need to ask God for help to overcome to be effective in this way?*

> "LET US NOT GIVE UP MEETING TOGETHER,
>   AS SOME ARE IN THE HABIT OF DOING,
>   BUT LET US ENCOURAGE
>   ONE ANOTHER—AND ALL THE MORE AS YOU
>   SEE THE DAY APPROACHING."
>   —HEBREWS 10:25

Chapter 5

WHAT I WISH MY YOUTH LEADER KNEW ABOUT . . .

MIDWEEK MEETINGS

I hate to admit it, but I don't always give the best first impression—especially at airports. Although I was born and raised in the U.S., I'm descended from Lebanese immigrants who came to America in the early 1900s. Because of that, I have black hair (which I like to wear long), a beard and a face reminiscent of people from the Middle East. Not usually a problem . . . until I go to airports.

Let me share with you a recent experience I had at Denver International Airport (DIA). I had just dropped off my wife for a trip to see her parents and was walking toward the exit of the newly opened terminal. I was in a hurry and frowning. (Wouldn't you frown if you'd just said good-bye to your spouse?)

> "I LIKE MY YOUTH GROUP'S MID-WEEK MEETING BECAUSE IT'S MORE FUNNER [SIC] AND I HAVE MORE FRIENDS IN THAT GROUP."
>
> —NINTH GRADER FROM A REFORMED CHURCH

That's when the "first impression" happened. A guard near the exit saw me, no luggage in hand, walking briskly toward the door. I passed him without thinking, only to be stopped seconds later by his command. Our conversation went something like this:

Guard: Hey, you! Come back here!

Me: *(Turning to make sure he was talking to me. He was.)* Me?

Guard: Yeah. *(A pause while he sizes me up. He weighs about 600 pounds more than me. It's no contest. His eyes narrow.)* Where are you from?

Me: *(Surprised.)* Colorado.

Guard: *(Annoyed.)* No. What country are you from?

Me: *(Starting to get annoyed myself.)* America.

Guard: No. Where were you born?

Me: Oklahoma.

Guard: *(In an accusatory tone.)* You look like you're from the Middle East. *(His exact words, I promise!)*

Me: *(Shrugging.)* Sorry.

Guard: *(Pausing to look me over again.)* You sure you're not from the Middle East? *(I shake my head.)* OK, you can go.

With that, I walked out. Unfortunately, I've had this kind of experience more than once—usually just after some terrorist attack that's made the headlines. The lesson I've learned? Given my appearance, I can give easily give the impression of the stereotypical Islamic terrorist.

I'm not the only one who can give a bad first impression. Consider Grammy-winning singer, Larnelle Harris. The first time he was to sing at a Billy Graham crusade, he arrived at the stadium a little late. He rushed to get to the stage for his scheduled sound check but was repeatedly denied entrance by well-meaning ushers who thought he was just trying to sneak in early for a good seat. One usher even accused him outright of lying, and started sharing the gospel in an effort to convert this obvious sinner![1]

Or consider the first impressions these job applicants gave when they wrote these employment-killing words on their résumés:[2]

"It's best for employers that I not work with people."

"References: None. I've left a path of destruction behind me."

"Instrumental in ruining entire operation for a Midwest chain store."

"Please don't misconstrue my 14 jobs as 'job-hopping.' I have never quit a job."

So why do I tell you about these mishaps in first impressions in a chapter on midweek youth meetings? Simple. For most teenagers in your community, the first impression they'll get of your youth group will be through a midweek meeting. That's where new kids are most likely to go to check out a youth group, and it's the meeting your existing youth group members are most likely to invite friends to attend.

Additionally, it's the midweek meeting that most often characterizes a teenager's description of a youth group as a whole. Because of that, it's vital we structure our weeknight meetings to present

"TWENTY YEARS AGO, THOSE MOST COMMITTED TO THEIR CHURCHES AVERAGED FOUR BLOCKS OF TIME DURING THE WEEK TO CORPORATE RELIGIOUS ACTIVITIES; TODAY, THE MOST COMMITTED CHURCH PEOPLE ALLOCATE TWO BLOCKS PER WEEK. WITH ONE OF THOSE BLOCKS TYPICALLY BEING THE SUNDAY MORNING WORSHIP SERVICE, THAT LEAVES ONLY ONE OTHER SEGMENT OF THEIR WEEKLY CALENDAR OPEN TO CHURCH-RELATED ACTIVITIES."

—DR. GEORGE BARNA[4]

an accurate reflection of what our ministries are all about and that we do so with teen interests and needs in mind. In short, it's important that our midweek meetings make a good "first impression" on the teenagers who attend them. Now, let's talk about how to do that.

Why Should I Come to Youth Group, Anyway?

> "JUST HAVE THE ABILITY TO RELATE TO TEENAGERS. TALK ON OUR LEVEL, BUT DON'T TALK DOWN TO US. TALK ABOUT THINGS WE UNDERSTAND AND CAN RELATE TO IN OUR EVERY-DAY LIVES AT SCHOOL AND EVERY-THING."
>
> —ELEVENTH-GRADE FEMALE FROM INDIANA

To begin, we need to know what draws students to our groups in the first place. When I asked teenagers for their reasons, the response was overwhelming: relationships. Three out of four young people surveyed indicated that cultivating a relationship with friends or cultivating a relationship with God was the primary reason they attended a youth group's weeknight meetings.

Now, I'd love to say that this desire to learn more about God was the number one response, but it wasn't. The top reason teenagers gave for coming to youth group during the week was "to see my friends." A whopping 40 percent of those surveyed chose this response—relegating a desire "to learn about God" (which pulled in 35% of the responses) to a strong second-place finish. To which I have to say: At least they're honest!

And, speaking of honesty, this emphasis on friendships is honestly not a surprise. InterVarsity Christian Fellowship campus staffer Andy Crouch sums the reason up when he says, "Building meaningful relationships matters to this generation, and the church can provide the ideal environment for young adults to find the 'human connection' they long for."[4]

GenX teenagers especially gravitate toward places that strengthen relationships. Remember, these are the last of the "latchkey kids" who spent much of childhood—and their present lives—fending for themselves while parents worked or partied without them. So the opportunity to see friends in a safe, upbeat environment becomes a big drawing card for teenagers.

That said, it's worth noting that there's an interesting "bell curve" when you break the numbers down by grade. Seventh graders are by far the least interested in "the friend factor," with only 13 percent saying that was their primary reason for going to a midweek meeting. In fact, that reason ranked behind three others among seventh graders, making them the only grade not to rank this choice in at least a tie for number one.

By eighth grade the number of students interested in connecting with friends more than doubles to 32 percent, or nearly one out of three kids. The friend factor grows even stronger for ninth graders, with 42 percent saying the primary reason they come to your youth group is to see their friends. And that number finally peaks in tenth grade, with nearly half (45%) citing that as their reason for coming. A healthy 43 percent of juniors and 35 percent of seniors come to a midweek meeting mainly to see their friends.

These numbers are significant because they represent a huge portion of our typical youth group members. Imagine if a pro football team lost 40 percent of its starters—about nine players in all—due to injury. It would cripple that team, changing a Super Bowl contender into a divisional has-been. Now imagine if your youth group lost 40 percent of its members due to a lack of emphasis on building friendships in your group. What

> "IF I COULD GIVE TEENAGERS ANY-
> THING, I'D GET THEM IN A CHURCH
> THAT HAS A GREAT YOUTH PRO-
> GRAM SO THAT THEY CAN GROW UP
> AND HAVE FELLOWSHIP WITH OTHER
> LIKE-MINDED BELIEVERS."
>
> —CARMAN[5]

would that leave you? Not much reason to hold a meeting, let alone run a youth ministry as a whole.

Although it's important to program for people relationships, we also need to remember the other significant reason our students attend a weeknight meeting: to learn about God. An almost equal number of guys (34%) and girls (35%) listed this as their primary reason for attending youth group.

So what does this mean? If you program for building relationships—both human and divine—you'll find you're meeting the needs of an overwhelming majority of your teenagers and giving them a reason to keep coming back as well.

Top Three Reasons Teenagers Give for Attending a Youth Group's Weeknight Meetings:

"To see my friends"	40%
"To learn about God"	35%
"To get advice for life"	13%

Percent of Teenagers Who Say the Primary Reason They Go to Youth Group Is "To See My Friends," by Grade:

Grade	Percentage	Where Ranked
7th Grade	13%	4
8th Grade	32%	1 (tie)
9th Grade	42%	1
10th Grade	45%	1
11th Grade	43%	1
12th Grade	35%	1 (tie)

Debunking a Few Myths

It's interesting to look at the things that are motivating teenagers to participate in weeknight meetings, but it's equally important to pay attention to what's *not* motivating them to come as well.

I was involved in a youth ministry once where an intern was convinced that the primary reason kids came to our midweek meeting was for the creative games we played. (We *did* play some pretty fun games!) His reasoning was that youth came on Sundays to study the Bible and on Tuesdays to play. As a result, our Tuesday night program refocused to concentrate more on game time and less on teaching time.

It took only a few months before this shift in philosophy took its toll. To put it bluntly, kids stopped coming. Our group drastically downsized from eighty or so regular attenders to less than ten. In all fairness, there were probably other factors at work too, but when we began to de-emphasize the games and reemphasize God, attendance began creeping upward again.

Our lesson? Kids like games as an appetizer, not as an entree. The results of this survey validate that lesson. In truth, only one of sixteen teenagers (6%) is coming to group simply for the fun and games. That's not to say games are unimportant or unwanted. In fact, nearly one in four teenagers (23%) rates the group games as the best part of their youth group's midweek meetings.

> "I THINK WITH [THE MIDWEEK MEETINGS AT] MY YOUTH GROUP, THE PASTOR TALKS A LOT AND IT GETS BORING. . . . I THINK FOR A YOUTH PASTOR TO BE A GOOD ONE, HE OR SHE NEEDS TO PLAN LOTS OF ACTIVITIES AND BE ORGANIZED. TELL A STORY EVERY WEEK AND NOT TALK ABOUT THE SAME THING ALL THE TIME. AND SOMETIMES THERE'S KIDS THAT DON'T LIKE TO SIT—BE PATIENT WITH THEM. YOUTH PASTORS SHOULD HAVE IT UNDER CONTROL. DON'T GET FRUSTRATED OR MAD WITH THE KIDS."
>
> —SEVENTH GRADER FROM NEW YORK

But those games *aren't* why these kids keep coming back. They're coming back to see their friends and to learn about God. That indicates that while games are important, an overemphasis on games doesn't meet our kids' needs in a weeknight meeting.

Another myth I often hear from youth leaders is this one: "These kids don't give a flying flip about anything. They're only here because their parents make them come."

Usually, this is given as an excuse for an unruly group or one that is stagnant in spiritual growth. But is this excuse really true? In a word, no.

Fact is, only one out of twenty youth group members (5%) goes to a midweek meeting because of his or her parents' insistence. To assume otherwise is to underestimate both our teenagers and our God who draws them there.

Now here's the statistic that really surprised me: Only one out of every *hundred* youth group members is attending a midweek meeting because you or I asked that person to come. That's right. Only one percent of teenagers says they go to a midweek youth meeting because a youth pastor asked them to go.

That could mean a couple of things. Perhaps we're not inviting as many kids to youth group as we think we are (though that seems unlikely to me), or perhaps our teenagers respond more to an invitation from their peers than from us. If that's the case, our best strategy is to capitalize on teen relationships and encourage kids we know to invite their friends to come to youth group.

INTERVIEWER: "HOW WOULD YOU IMPROVE YOUR YOUTH GROUP'S MIDWEEK MEETINGS?" FEMALE TENTH GRADER FROM A LUTHERAN CHURCH: "BY MAKING THEM AT A MORE CONVENIENT TIME."

REASONS LEAST LIKELY TO MOTIVATE A TEENAGER TO ATTEND A YOUTH GROUP'S WEEKNIGHT MEETING:

"My youth leader asks me to go"	1%
"My parents make me"	5%
"To play fun group games"	6%

When and What?

Now that we know why young people attend a midweek youth meeting—and why they don't—the natural questions that follow are when to schedule those midweek meetings and what to do during them.

The answer to the first question is easy. For nearly two-thirds of our teenagers, Wednesday still rates as the "best night for a midweek meeting." If you held meetings on every other weeknight except Wednesday, you'd still attract just over half as many kids as you'd get on an average Wednesday night. Of all nights to avoid, Friday is the worst.

"THE BEST ADVICE I COULD GIVE A YOUTH PASTOR IS, WITH TEENS, TO GO AND LET THEM EXPERIENCE THINGS THEMSELVES. BRING IT DOWN TO THEIR LEVEL OF KNOWLEDGE AND REALIZE THEY TAKE MORE TIME TO UNDERSTAND THINGS, AND THAT THEY NEED AS MUCH HELP AND INFLUENCE AS THEY CAN GET."

—TWELFTH-GRADE FEMALE FROM A LUTHERAN CHURCH

Typically reserved for dates and school sporting events, Friday night offers the most competition to a weeknight youth meeting.

Once kids have come to a midweek meeting, what parts of the programming are they enjoying? With one of every three students (33%) rating group discussion as "the best part of the programming" in their youth group's weeknight meetings, this choice was easily the number one response among teenagers surveyed. Given kids' desire to connect with friends, this should come as no surprise. Few things can facilitate relationships more quickly than simply talking to others.

As I mentioned earlier, group games are still fun for our teenagers—especially among eighth and ninth graders. Students in these grades rated their youth group's games as the number one thing they enjoyed about the programming of the midweek meetings they currently attend. Interestingly enough, more than one-fourth of the ninth graders chose group games as the best part of these meetings—but only one out of fifty (2%) says those games are the primary reason they attend their group.

Group singing also pulled in some support, with about one in six students (17%) saying this was the best part of their midweek meeting.

Now let's look at what teens enjoy least about our midweek meetings: the teaching time (which ranked dead last) and the prayer time (which ranked second to last by a slim margin).

Unfortunately, this is a sad commentary on the state of our midweek meetings. Arguably the two most important facets of a youth group meeting are the two things our teenagers find to be the least enjoyable parts of our program.

Surprisingly, youth leaders themselves ranked the teaching time in the top two among programming they thought teenagers liked best at a midweek meeting—a perception that is clearly out of sync with what teenagers truly believe. Equally surprising, not one youth leader listed "the prayer time" as something teenagers like best at a midweek meeting. Both these results are disappointing, to say the least. The first suggests we're blind to how poor our teaching really is, and the second suggests our prayer time during a midweek meeting (if we have any) is not connecting with teenagers.

This is especially disheartening when you consider that our teaching and prayer times are designed to lead kids into deeper relationship with God—and that a deeper relationship with God is precisely the reason more than one-third of our teenagers attend our midweek meetings.

In our Bible schools and seminaries we're supposedly taught in great detail how to prepare attention-grabbing, life-changing sermons. We're also taught to become great men and women of prayer and to pass those prayer habits on to our teenagers. Somewhere, we've fallen short.

I have no easy answers for how to reverse this negative perception of our teaching and prayer times. Suffice it to say at this point that we're sorely lacking in these two areas. God help us if we don't find a way to improve.

"WHICH IS THE BEST NIGHT FOR A WEEKNIGHT MEETING?"

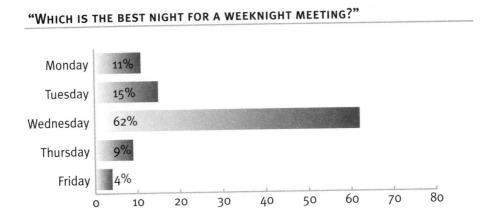

Monday	11%
Tuesday	15%
Wednesday	62%
Thursday	9%
Friday	4%

0 10 20 30 40 50 60 70 80

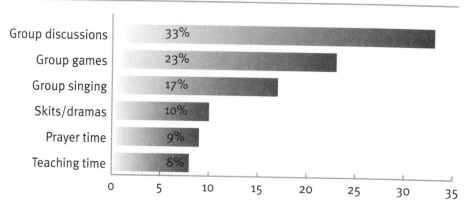

"WHAT'S THE BEST PART OF THE PROGRAMMING IN YOUR YOUTH GROUP'S WEEKNIGHT MEETINGS?"

Group discussions	33%
Group games	23%
Group singing	17%
Skits/dramas	10%
Prayer time	9%
Teaching time	8%

0   5   10   15   20   25   30   35

Chapter Summary and Observations

The primary reasons teenagers come to midweek meetings are to see friends and to learn about God.

That means we need to be proactive about programming for relationships. Seek opportunities to bring teenagers together. Use discussion groups. Try "community builder" or "team encouragement" activities regularly. Facilitate open sharing and provide a safe environment where that sharing can happen. In short, think of the students who attend your midweek meetings as a "family" and encourage them to adopt that attitude as well.

Additionally, don't cut God short. Your teenagers really do want to know more about Jesus, so don't apologize for helping them in this area. Instead, insist on including meaningful opportunities for your kids to deepen their relationship with God through prayer and Scripture.

> "AS ARTISTS GIVE THEMSELVES TO THEIR MODELS, AND POETS TO THEIR CLASSICAL PURSUITS, SO MUST WE ADDICT OURSELVES TO PRAYER."
> —CHARLES SPURGEON[6]

Finally, cultivate your own personal friendships with kids in your community. Perhaps then your invitation to a midweek meeting will mean something to teenagers.

For the most part, a parent's coercion rarely motivates teenagers to attend your weeknight meetings.

If a young person really, truly doesn't want to come to youth group, sooner or later that person will find a way out. When you assume a parent's insistence is the sole attendance motivation among kids in your group, you cheapen your efforts to reach them and cheat both the teenagers and God out of opportunities for spiritual growth.

Even among teenagers who display a negative attitude about church and who say they're only there because a parent makes them come, you must assume more. You must assume that: 1) God has brought that student, regardless of what that student claims, and 2) somewhere inside, that student is secretly hoping you'll give him or her a new reason for coming—a reason that can be found only in a relationship with Jesus Christ.

Wednesday night is by far the best night for teenagers to attend a midweek meeting.

'Nuff said.

We need to work much harder at making our teaching and prayer times meaningful for students.

Perhaps the first step in rectifying this situation is for us to spend more time on our knees ourselves. We can only teach out of the overflow of our own spiritual growth. If we're not making personal time with God a priority, it will show in our teaching and become a habit that our teenagers imitate.

We would also do well to find ways to vary our teaching style, to incorporate more discussion time and to include teenagers themselves in leading the teaching and prayer times of a midweek meeting. Whatever we do, we must do it quickly. Our time with these teenagers is a precious commodity. We can't afford to waste another day—or another midweek meeting.

For Personal Reflection

Take a few moments now to process your own reaction to the information in this chapter. Use these questions to help spark your thinking:

- *What suspicions about midweek meetings did you have confirmed by the information in this chapter? What surprised you?*

- *What specific things can you do this week to program for relationships in your midweek meetings?*

- *Why do you suppose our teaching and prayer times are not "the best part" of our midweek meetings? What can you do about that?*

Chapter 6

WHAT I WISH MY YOUTH LEADER KNEW ABOUT . . .

SMALL GROUPS

The lights dimmed. The big screen flickered, then came to life. The audience at the Toronto Film Festival settled in to watch Robert Duvall's "baby," the movie *The Apostle*. Scattered throughout the audience were executives from several big-league motion picture companies. For Duvall, everything counted on this screening and on those executives.

Robert Duvall was well-known in film circles. During his thirty-five-year career he earned a Best Actor Oscar award for his performance in 1983's *Tender Mercies* and a handful of other Oscar nominations for performances in movies such as *The Godfather* and *Apocalypse Now*. But when he wanted to make a movie about a fallen preacher looking for redemption, studio executives passed on the idea.

Undaunted, Duvall went ahead and wrote the screenplay. And directed the movie. And starred in it. And spent $5 million of his own money to produce the film. By the time of the Toronto showing, the stakes were sky-high. Duvall's only hope of recovering that money would be if at least one of the motion picture companies represented in the audience thought *The*

> "A LEADER WHO CAN NURTURE A GROUP OF STUDENTS WILL EXPERIENCE A DEPTH OF MINISTRY NEVER REACHED IN JUST BEING UP FRONT AND RUNNING THE SHOW."
>
> —DOUG FIELDS[1]

Apostle was a valuable enough property to purchase rights to distribute it to the movie-going public.

So Duvall waited.

The movie kept rolling. In the dark it was hard to gauge the kind of response it was getting.

Suddenly, not even halfway through the screening, a few of the "suits" had had enough. Executives from Miramax and October Films gathered their things and headed for the door! All indications were that they were giving up on the film, not even interested enough to see it through to the end.

Reality, however, can sometimes surprise you. Moments after these executives left the theater, Duvall's phone rang. Then it rang again. Both Miramax and October Films had liked the film so much they rushed out to be the first ones to make the deal for Duvall's film. A bidding war erupted between the two studios, finally ending around 1:00 A.M.

> "SOME TEENAGERS DON'T PARTICI-
> PATE IN SMALL GROUPS BECAUSE
> THEY SEE MANY GROUPS AS
> CLIQUES AND THEY'RE AFRAID OF
> WHAT OTHERS WILL THINK OF THEM.
> WE NEED TO BE MORE OPEN WITH
> OTHERS IN THE GROUP."
> — TWELFTH GRADER FROM ILLINOIS

When all was said and done, October Films walked away with rights to distribute *The Apostle* worldwide, and Robert Duvall walked away with a check for $6 million—a cool million in profit— and the potential to make much more.[2]

Sometimes a small-group program within a youth ministry can seem like a movie nobody wants. Like Robert Duvall you invest time, energy and resources into creating a small-group ministry that kids will love—only to see them respond with apathy and feigned disinterest.

Do you give up there? I don't think so. Doug Fields, youth pastor at Saddleback Church in southern California, points out that small groups in a youth ministry have several benefits. According to Fields, "Small groups allow students to be known . . . make students verbal . . . allow students to personalize their faith . . . [and] encourage accountable relationships."[3]

Bo Boshers, high school pastor at Willow Creek Community Church in Illinois, agrees. He asserts that "small groups maximize life change, stop program-driven ministry, keep the ministry small in bigness, disciple leaders and students, and build community."[4]

> "THE GOAL OF COMMUNITY IS TO KNIT GROUP MEMBERS TOGETHER IN LOVE AND TO BUILD THEM AS WHOLE PEOPLE. THIS HAPPENS AS PEOPLE SHARE NEEDS, CONFESS SINS AND FAULTS, BEAR EACH OTHER'S BURDENS, HELP OTHERS IDENTIFY AND DEVELOP THEIR SPIRITUAL GIFTS, ENCOURAGE EACH OTHER, LISTEN CAREFULLY AND INTERCEDE IN PRAYER."
> —RON NICHOLAS[5]

Imagine what might have happened if Robert Duvall had stopped the screening of *The Apostle* at the midpoint, said "Aah, nobody's interested anyway," and filed his movie—and his money—in the trash bin. He would never have seen the rewards of his efforts or found out the true value of his film.

Likewise, if we give up on small groups, we lose all the benefits associated with them. And just as the movie studio executives valued *The Apostle* enough to skip the ending, your teenagers actually *do* value small groups—perhaps more than you think. Let me show you what I mean.

What Teenagers Really Think About Small Groups

Researcher Dr. George Barna reports that only about 12 percent of adult churchgoers attend small-group meetings in a given week.[6] By contrast, Barna reports that more than double that number of youth (25%) attend a small-group Bible study for teenagers. He explains, "Often, these groups appeal to teens because of the relational opportunities."[7]

But even those healthy numbers don't show how highly your teenagers actually value a small-group program in your youth ministry. In reality, more than 70 percent of teenagers rate small groups in a youth group as either "very important" or "moderately important." Only one out of every ten students sees small groups as "not important at all."

INTERVIEWER: "WHY DO YOU SUP-
POSE MANY TEENAGERS ARE RELUC-
TANT TO PARTICIPATE IN SMALL
GROUPS?"
NINTH GRADER FROM A REFORMED
CHURCH: "BECAUSE THEY THINK IT'S
BORING AND THERE AREN'T MANY
INTERESTING TOPICS, AND IT'S ALL
BIBLE READING AND NO FUN."

Not surprisingly, students in high school seem to value small groups more than those in junior high. Among seventh graders, only one in five (20%) rates small groups as "very important." About one in six eighth graders (17%) rates small groups that way.

For grades nine through twelve, though, roughly one in three (30%) students considers small groups "very important." Sophomores placed by far the highest value on small groups, with a whopping 40 percent rating them that high. Seniors are the second-most likely group to value small groups highly, with 27 percent rating them as very important.

Looking at all grades as a whole, girls are much more likely to value strongly a small-group structure than are guys. Thirty-two percent of the young women gave small groups the highest possible rating, compared to only 23 percent of guys—a difference of nearly ten full percentage points.

Of course, with one in four guys placing this high a value on small groups, it would be premature to assume guys are uninterested in small-group involvement. Still, only rarely in this survey did gender make that much of a difference regarding a specific question or topic.

Now for the bad news. For every student who rated small groups as "very important," an equal number of group members (29%) rated small groups as only "slightly important" or "not important at all." With some fluctuation, these percentages stayed pretty consistent regardless of age or gender. On the whole, kids in seventh and eighth grade were *most* likely to choose one of these responses, and students in eleventh and twelfth grades were *least* likely.

Generally speaking, then, we must assume that no matter what we do with small groups in our ministry, there will always be a core of students who just aren't interested. For those kids we'll have to do our best to make our other youth group programs enriching enough to provide a substantive basis for spiritual growth. Meanwhile, we can take comfort in knowing that the vast majority of our teenagers do indeed value a small-group experience, and that makes it all worthwhile.

> "SMALL GROUPS ARE MADE UP OF PEOPLE EACH OF WHOM IS DIFFERENT. EACH COMES TO THE GROUP WITH EXPECTATIONS, FEARS, BACKGROUNDS, PERSONALITIES—ALL DIFFERENT. "AS LEADERS, OUR GOAL IS TO BRING THIS DIVERSITY INTO A CLOSE-KNIT UNITY. THAT IS NOT EASY."
>
> —JUDY JOHNSON[8]

"HOW IMPORTANT TO YOU ARE SMALL GROUPS IN A YOUTH GROUP?"

Very important: 29%
Moderately important: 42%
Slightly important: 19%
Not important at all: 10%

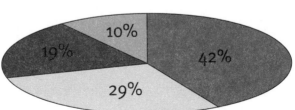

PERCENT OF TEENAGERS WHO RATE SMALL GROUPS AS "VERY IMPORTANT" IN A YOUTH MINISTRY, BY GRADE AND GENDER

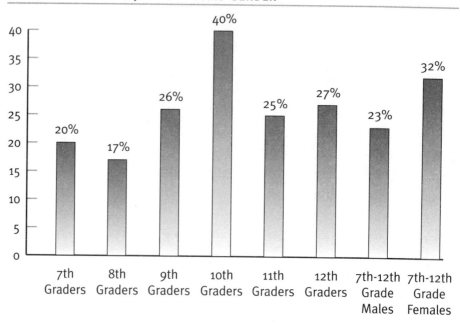

To Get Involved or Not to Get Involved, That Is the Question

After digging through the solid, yet unspectacular data on how important teenagers feel small groups are, I expected no significantly new information regarding kids' feelings about their levels of involvement in said groups. Boy, was I in for a surprise!

While 71 percent of teenagers gave small groups a "very important" or "moderately important" rating, a full 86 percent indicated they are either comfortable with their current level of involvement in a small group or would actually like to become *more* involved in a small group. With that kind of approval rating, we must be doing something right in our small-group ministries. (Go ahead and congratulate yourself.)

This becomes more interesting when you compare the number of teenagers who desire greater involvement with those who desire less or no involvement. In almost every case (eighth graders being the only exception), for each young person who wants out of a small group, there are two (or more) who want in!

Now let's glance back at the importance ratings seventh graders gave to small groups. With 27 percent of these kids rating small groups as "not important at all," you'd think they'd also be the grade that's least interested in becoming more involved in a small group. At least that's what I thought, but I was wrong—dead wrong.

Truth is, *more than half* the seventh graders surveyed (53%) indicated a desire for greater involvement in a small group. Seventh graders aren't the only group with that large a number of students requesting opportunity for more involvement. Exactly half of the juniors surveyed said they wanted more, and two-fifths of seniors said the same thing. Overall, 41 percent of all our teenagers are craving more in the way of small groups.

INTERVIEWER: "WHY DO YOU SUP-POSE MANY TEENAGERS ARE RELUCTANT TO PARTICIPATE IN SMALL GROUPS?" METHODIST TENTH GRADER FROM TEXAS: "PROBABLY, LIKE FOR ME, THEY'RE WORRIED ABOUT WHAT OTHER PEOPLE THINK AND MAYBE THEY'RE ALSO AFRAID OF GETTING CLOSE TO GOD."

Folks, these numbers are huge! Imagine how Coca-Cola® would respond if a survey revealed to them that half of Americans wanted more of their products? Or how McDonald's would act if it became known that 40 percent of their patrons wanted more Big Mac™-related foods? We'd be ordering Coke®-milkshakes to go along with our Big-Mac™-McMuffins™ in no time!

For us as youth leaders, the window of opportunity is open so wide here it's blinding. But we can't assume we'll have this opportunity forever.

We have the privilege to be ministers at a unique moment when teenagers not only need but want to be more involved in the community a small group brings. It's our duty, then, to provide a place where

> "HATE IS REPLACED ONLY BY LOVE
> AND BY COMMUNITY."
> —SISTER HELEN PREJEAN[9]

those small-group communities can flourish to last through this generation and thrive in generations beyond as well. If we miss that opportunity, we deserve the negative consequences that failure would bring.

Let me share a story from history to help bring home this point. In 1269, the great Mongol leader, Kublai Khan, sent a request from Peking to the pope in Rome asking for "a hundred wise men in the Christian religion." The request went further to state that Khan had decided to become a Christian, desired to be baptized and, as was the custom of his day, wished to pass on his new faith to his country and its leaders. "There will be more Christians here than there are in your parts," Khan's letter promised.

Pope Gregory X received the request but thought little of it. Instead of sending a hundred wise Christians, he sent merely two Dominican friars. Those two friars might still have been enough, but we'll never know. Partway through their journey to Peking, they gave up and returned to Rome instead. The would-be Christian, Kublai Khan, sat waiting in Asia for no one.[10]

Although it's impossible to tell what may have happened had Pope Gregory X seized the moment before him, we can safely say that he missed a great opportunity to impact a great number of people and potentially change the course of history in Asia and the world.

We have a similar "impact moment" before us now. We have large numbers of teenagers who want to be a part of a small-group ministry. It's up to us to do something about it.

"IN REGARD TO SMALL GROUPS, I WOULD LIKE TO . . ."

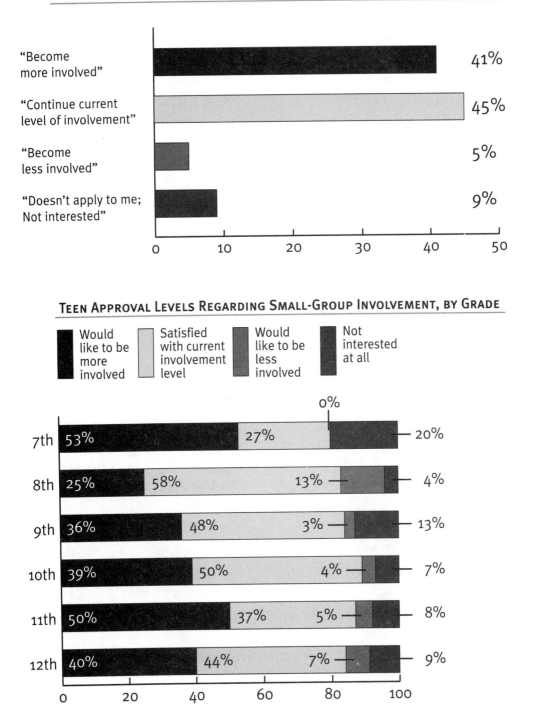

TEEN APPROVAL LEVELS REGARDING SMALL-GROUP INVOLVEMENT, BY GRADE

Community Seekers

We know that our teenagers want small groups, and we know they want to be more involved in small groups, but what exactly do our teenagers want *from* a small group? What purpose do they see for a small group's existence?

The answer is simple: They want a community of believers committed to each other and to God.

Consider this: When asked to identify the "main purpose" of a small group, the top three choices of teenagers all had to do with community functions. The number one choice by far was "To deepen relationships with other Christians." Number two was "To challenge the members of the small group to grow spiritually." Following close behind at number three was "to create a support group for the members of the small group."

> "I'M ALWAYS LOOKING AT THINGS AND GOING, 'HOW CAN WE DO THAT BETTER? HOW CAN WE CHANGE THIS? HOW CAN WE GROW A BIGGER VISION? HOW CAN WE REACH MORE KIDS? HOW CAN WE DO THIS IN A WAY THAT'S NEVER BEEN DONE BEFORE?'"
>
> —SUSIE SHELLENBERGER[11]

Break the numbers down by gender and you get the same results from both females and males. Separate the numbers by grade and, with the exception of ninth graders, these three choices still fall in the same slots. (Ninth graders ranked "a support group" at number one, and "deepen relationships" at number three.)

What about traditional purposes for small groups such as Bible study, prayer and evangelism? These emphases barely registered a blip on the radar screen. Evangelism especially ranked low, with only 3 percent of teenagers saying this should be a "main purpose" of a small group.

Why the low marks for these things? My general feel isn't that our teenagers regard them as unimportant but that they see these particular needs met in other arenas of the youth ministry program.

Some measure of Bible study and prayer happens at Sunday school and midweek meetings. Evangelism happens at school. But for 80 percent of these teenagers, Christian community happens mainly in the small group. Because of that, a small group is where they expect to deepen relationships, build support groups and challenge each other to new spiritual heights.

Our students crave this kind of community. They've grown up in a nation where divorce is the norm, both parents working outside the home is expected and they've been largely left to fend for themselves. These kids, however, care about relationships and care about each other. They, of all people, have the potential to truly build a healthy small group of interdependent Christian teenagers.

> "I NEED YOU. THIS IS SUCH A DIFFICULT AND STRESSFUL TIME IN MY LIFE, I NEED SOMEONE TO LOVE ME AND SUPPORT ME AND GIVE ME STRENGTH. I PROMISE I WILL DO THE SAME FOR YOU."
> —FIFTEEN-YEAR-OLD FEMALE[12]

And we get to help.

"THE MAIN PURPOSE OF A SMALL GROUP SHOULD BE . . ."

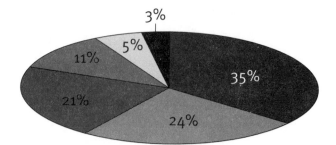

"To deepen relationships with other Christians."   35%

"To challenge the members of the small group to grow spiritually."   24%

"To create a support group for the members of the small group."   21%

"To study the Bible more in-depth."   11%

"To pray for the members of the small group."   5%

"To evangelize or help others become Christians."   3%

Chapter Summary and Observations

Generally speaking, our teenagers regard small groups as an important part of a youth ministry.

This is good news, because it means they value this essential part of your ministry. The bad news is that thinking of small groups as important doesn't guarantee your teenagers will be consistent in attending those groups.

If that seems to be the case in your ministry, remember that availability is sometimes as important as appropriation. By this I mean that for many teenagers, just knowing the group is available to them when they need it is an emotional plus—whether their attendance is erratic or not. In fact, if Dr. George Barna is correct (and I believe he is), we can probably expect our young people to be inconsistent in attendance rather than the opposite. It's a new cultural reality to which we must learn to adapt.[13]

That said, we can't lose sight of the fact that the vast majority of our teenagers still value small groups. Therefore, we need to be diligent to invest in these groups by recruiting and training leaders, scheduling regular small-group meetings and supporting them publicly in our other areas of ministry. It would also be wise for you to participate in an adult small group as well, showing by example that you also value a small-group ministry.

Large numbers of our teenagers desire greater involvement in small groups the youth ministry provides.

This is great news, because at present only one in four of our kids is actively involved in a small group. We must take advantage of this current interest and increase the profile and ministry of teenage small groups in our churches.

If you don't have small groups, start a few. Utilize small groups during discussion times at Sunday school and midweek meetings, and encourage kids to stay in those same groups from week to week. Take advantage of the flexibility and mobility of existing small groups to plan "small group only" events. Make it easy for students to find out when and where small groups are happening; perhaps a poster in the youth room or a weekly flyer would facilitate that.

In short, do everything you can to make small-group involvement something that's easy and accessible for your youth group members.

Four out of five teenagers are looking for a small group to provide a sense of Christian community among its members.

I'm told that among first-century Christians, nonbelievers would shake their heads in wonder and often proclaim, "See how these Christians love each other!" Funny thing is, that assessment could be used to describe many of the teenagers we minister to today.

Not long ago, I sat in my church during a Sunday morning sermon. When the time came for prayer, one of the teen girls from my small group knelt at the altar for prayer. Before my wife could make her way down to the front to pray with her, that student was encircled by a half dozen other girls who wanted to support her in prayer. My wife actually had to elbow her way into the crowd!

Those girls loved each other, and that love took root and grew through community created by meeting each week in a small group. Your teenagers are ripe for that kind of community. Give it to them through the way you structure your small-group ministry; enable them to deepen relationships, challenge each other to grow and support each other through thick and thin. Believe me, we'll all be glad you did.

For Personal Reflection

Take a few moments now to process your own reaction to the information in this chapter. Use these questions to help spark your thinking:

- *Why do you suppose teenagers tend to value the small-group environment?*

- *If it's true that a significant portion of your teenagers desire to be more involved in a small group, what can you do to take advantage of that truth?*

- *What would you say characterizes a healthy "Christian community"? How can you incorporate those characteristics in your small-group program?*

*"AFTER SIX DAYS JESUS TOOK PETER,
JAMES AND JOHN WITH HIM AND LED
THEM UP A HIGH MOUNTAIN, WHERE THEY
WERE ALL ALONE. THERE HE WAS
TRANSFIGURED BEFORE THEM."*
—MARK 9:2

Chapter 7

WHAT I WISH MY YOUTH LEADER KNEW ABOUT . . .

CAMPS AND RETREATS

Charlie was just another squirrelly kid in grade school when God came calling. He had joined his friends from church for a week-long camp in upstate New York. The camp had a western theme, so Charlie spent plenty of time playing in the great outdoors, riding horses, feasting at cookouts and more.

But one night during the camp, the leaders put on a puppet show and explained how a kid like Charlie could trust in Jesus for forgiveness of sin. He asked a camp counselor for help, and together they went outside. It was there, on a dusty lane in the midst of a mock western town, that Charlie gave his life to Jesus.

Several years later that decision to follow Christ prompted Charlie to become active in his church's youth group, then a leader in that group as well. He and some of his high school buddies went to college together, and it was there they formed a Christian band.

Today, Charlie Lowell is still in that band as one-fourth of the award-winning group,

FROM A CARTOON BY JOHN MCPHERSON:

"YOU'RE ON A YOUTH RETREAT WHEN A KID PUTS A MILDLY POISONOUS SNAKE DOWN YOUR SHIRT. DO YOU:

A. ASSIGN HIM 24 HOURS OF LATRINE DUTY,

B. SEND HIM HOME AND RECOMMEND HARSH DISCIPLINE, OR

C. LAUGH IT OFF AS JUST A HARMLESS PRANK?"[1]

Jars of Clay. Together with his band-mates, they've toured the world, created hit song after hit song, and impacted millions with the message of Jesus Christ. And for Charlie, it all started at a "cowboy camp" where a counselor like you took a few moments to pray with him to accept Christ in his heart.[2]

Paul absolutely, positively did *not* want to go. So what if those church freaks were going to spend a weekend at a retreat center in the woods of New Hampshire? There was *no way* Paul was going. God was the last thing on his mind. So this teenager gave the youth leader who had invited him a thanks-but-no-thanks speech and went merrily on his way.

"I AM CONVINCED OF THE EFFEC-TIVENESS OF RETREATS. OVER THE COURSE OF MY EXPERIENCE IN YOUTH MINISTRY, I HAVE SEEN MORE HAPPEN IN THE LIVES OF STU-DENTS ON RETREATS THAN ALMOST ANYWHERE ELSE.

"RETREATS ARE EXCELLENT FOR BUILDING GROUP IDENTITY, CHAL-LENGING STUDENTS WITH THE CLAIMS OF CHRIST, AND FOLLOWING UP ON DISCIPLESHIP RELATION-SHIPS. RETREATS GIVE YOUTH LEAD-ERS A CONCENTRATED OPPORTUNI-TY FOR LEADING STUDENTS TO A RELATIONSHIP WITH CHRIST, EVEN AS THESE STUDENTS ARE ABLE TO EXPERIENCE HIS LOVE THROUGH THE RELATIONSHIPS OF THE MINI-COM-MUNITY THAT CAN BE FORMED ON A RETREAT."

—PAUL BORTHWICK[4]

A few days later, the youth leader again invited him to come. Paul refused. The leader invited him again. And again. And just about every time he came into contact with this wayward teen. To make things worse, Paul's parents got into the act, urging him to spend the weekend on the retreat.

Finally, Paul reasoned, "Well, the cute girls are enough to make up for the boring Bible studies," and he consented to go.

But something unexpected happened on that retreat. Here's how Paul describes it:

"God was at work on that retreat. Through the prayers of others and the working of the Holy Spirit in me, I came to a point of self-evaluation on the retreat. In the quietness of the New Hampshire woods, I came to see that God had a higher purpose for my life and that I could not outrun him. My life was changed on that retreat."[3]

Years later, Paul Borthwick became one of those youth leaders who persistently love kids into the kingdom of God. Through his writing, he also became a pioneering voice for youth ministry in the 1980s, influencing thousands of youth leaders and, through them, hundreds of thousands of teenagers as well. If you studied youth ministry in college, you may have even read one of his books as a textbook!

And it all started at a weekend retreat in the beauty of a New Hampshire wilderness.

It's obvious why I tell you these stories. We can never underestimate the impact a simple summer camp or weekend retreat can have, not only on the students in our group but also on every person our teenagers touch *after* that camp or retreat. And we need to remember that hidden within those kids who come to our camps are untold numbers of Charlie Lowells and Paul Borthwicks.

> "FOR OUR YOUTH GROUP, RETREATS TEACH YOU SO MUCH! IT'S A DIFFERENT PERSON SPEAKING TO YOU THAN YOUR PASTOR AND THEY COME IN AND TELL STORIES. IT'S GOOD TO GET AWAY FROM HOME TOO. THEY'RE LOTS OF FUN AND HAVE LOTS OF ACTIVITIES. IT'S GOOD THAT ONCE OR TWICE A YEAR, YOUR YOUTH GROUP GOES ON A RETREAT."
> —SEVENTH GRADER FROM NEW YORK

Thankfully, camps and retreats are a standard staple in ministry to teenagers, and you're probably an old veteran at pulling these kinds of trips off! But how effective are these outings? What do our kids really like (and dislike) during a camp or retreat? And, honestly, what are they willing to spend for these experiences? Let's find out.

Investments and Returns

Veteran youth pastor Von Trutzschler loves to use object lessons to make his point. One of his classics is when he walks into a youth room carrying a ragged section of newspaper.

"This old paper has REAL value," Von will say. "Who knows? It may contain information or reveal a secret worth millions!"

Next he'll try to give the paper to some unlucky soul. He'll ramble on about the paper's potential worth and practically beg some teen to take it off his hands. It's a low investment for the teenagers—just take the paper and either keep it or throw it away. Still, Von reports that no one is ever willing to make that minor investment.

Then he reveals his secret: He has taped a $10 bill inside the moldy newsprint. Whoever took the paper would have gotten the cash in return![5]

Now, it is true that a youth camp or retreat is significantly more investment than simply taking ownership of a newspaper, but the return on that investment is financially immeasurable. Here's why:

For every ten teenagers who attend a youth camp or retreat, *seven* of them will make a life-changing decision that will have a lasting positive effect on their relationship with God.

"I THINK A LOT OF SMALL CHURCHES LIKE THE ONE I GO TO DON'T HAVE ENOUGH MONEY OR PEOPLE INVOLVED TO DO THE KINDS OF THINGS THEY WANT, SO THEY SEND THEIR KIDS TO RETREATS AS AN ALTERNATIVE."

—NINTH-GRADE METHODIST

I asked the participants in our survey this simple yes-or-no question, "Have you ever made a life-changing decision at a camp or retreat that continues to have a positive impact on your relationship with God today?"

I wanted to discover two things with this question: 1) did they make a decision they considered life-changing during a camp or retreat; and 2) did that decision make a lasting impact?

I had anticipated about half of the teenagers responding positively. In reality, 71 percent of those teens surveyed answered "yes" to that question. Wow!

Let's put this in perspective a bit. What would you do if your bank offered you a savings account that yielded a 70 percent return? The answer is obvious—you'd be crazy not to invest in that account.

Or what if a car salesperson sold seven out of every ten cars he or she showed to a customer? That salesperson would soon own a fleet of car dealerships and have millions in the bank as well.

These numbers indicate a few things to me. First, we plant and water quite a bit during our typical "at-home" youth ministry—that is, during Sunday school, midweek meetings, small groups, worship times, special events and service projects. But when it comes time to harvest, much of that exciting work happens in a camp or a retreat setting.

> "RELATIONSHIPS ARE CENTRAL AT CAMP BECAUSE OUR GOD IS A RELATIONAL GOD. BEFORE ANYTHING ELSE WAS, GOD WAS AND IS THREE PERSONS: FATHER, SON, AND HOLY SPIRIT. THEREFORE WHEN WE CAMP TOGETHER, WE ENJOY A DOUBLE DIVINE CONTEXT: CREATION, WHICH DECLARES THE GLORY OF GOD, AND COMMUNITY, WHICH DECLARES THE RELATIONAL NATURE OF GOD."
>
> —AL MCKAY AND R. PAUL STEVENS[6]

I wouldn't think it wise to assume that camps are more important than at-home ministry activities. Rather, my feeling is that camps and retreats are the natural culmination of our efforts to plant and water God's Word in the hearts of the teenagers in our care.

The second thing I notice is that we can't afford to put on second-rate camps. For youth leaders, a camp is like the Christmas season for retailers. A department store will take in 50 percent or more of its annual sales in the month of December. Because of that, stores go all out to give their Christmas products the best possible chances of being sold by hawking sales, creating eye-popping ad campaigns and more.

If our camps and retreats afford us the best possible opportunity to lead our students into life-changing decisions for Christ, we need to give our best efforts to making them top-quality.

Please don't misunderstand. I'm not suggesting we start holding retreats in five-star hotels and serving gourmet food for lunch. But I am suggesting that the next camp or retreat you put on deserves ample time in creative planning, preparation and prayer. To throw together a "good enough" retreat at the last minute shortchanges our ministry and our students.

Now let me clarify that not every retreat or camp will always yield seven new Christians—though that could happen. More often you'll get to witness a deepening of a relationship with Christ in your teenagers, or a recommitment from a straying teen, or a desire to follow a certain aspect of God's will—all of which can be life-changing for a young person. Additionally, since teens often attend more than one camp during their time in your youth group, you may see the impact on teenagers staggered from camp to camp.

Which leads to the question, When we're planning a camp or retreat, what kinds of things are best to include? Let's see what we can discover from the survey responses.

"HAVE YOU EVER MADE A LIFE-CHANGING DECISION AT A CAMP OR RETREAT THAT CONTINUES TO HAVE A POSITIVE IMPACT ON YOUR RELATIONSHIP WITH GOD TODAY?"

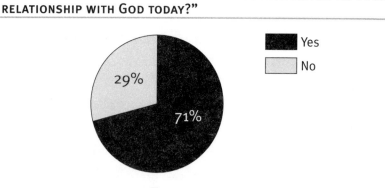

What I Like About Camp!

With input from other youth leaders, I compiled a list of eleven basic elements of a church-camp experience. Then I asked teenagers to choose the top two elements they liked best about a camp or retreat. The results were heartening, as kids strongly favored what I believe are the three primary purposes of hosting an outing like this.

The number one thing (by a whisker!) that young people like about a retreat or camp is gaining an opportunity for a more in-depth exploration of God. Over two-fifths of teenagers (42%) chose this response.

In explaining why this is such a highlight of camps, one senior from Missouri said, "I think that kids nowadays need to . . . learn more about the Bible. They need to be able to show it in the world." And for this young man, a retreat provides an opportunity to meet that need—which is all the reason he needs to go on one.

INTERVIEWER: "WHY DO YOU THINK CAMPS AND RETREATS HAVE BECOME SUCH A VITAL PART OF A TYPICAL YOUTH MINISTRY SCHEDULE?"
NINTH GRADER FROM PENNSYLVANIA: "PROBABLY SO IT'S A DIFFERENT ENVIRONMENT FOR KIDS TO GET AWAY TO AND EXPERIENCE NEW THINGS —AND ALSO REALIZE HOW CHRIST IS CHANGING OTHERS' LIVES TOO."

The second element your youth group likes about a camp or retreat is "building deeper friendships." This choice scored so strongly (41%) that it very nearly took the number one spot.

It's important to note, however, that when you factor in a few percentage points for a standard margin of error with any survey, it's entirely possible that building deeper friendships could be the true number one factor kids like best. We'll never know for sure, so for now I'll stick with this one as a strong second.

With that in mind, let me reiterate something that seems to be a recurring theme throughout this book:

Relationships! Relationships! Relationships!

Did I mention that your teenagers—both GenX and Millennial Gen—value relationships *very* highly? No matter what the category, no matter what the subject, no matter what the choices, the one thing this survey keeps hammering home is that relationships must be our highest programming priority in every aspect of our ministry to teenagers. Camps and retreats are no exception.

The great thing is that a camp or retreat is inherently good at deepening relationships. Students and leaders are forced to eat, drink, sleep, play, study, learn, worship and live in close proximity the entire time. You can't spend this much time with people without some kind of relationship benefit.

> "I THINK [YOUNG LIFE HAS] THE PREMIER CAMPING PROPERTIES IN THE WORLD, WHEN IT COMES TO YOUTH MINISTRY. AND THAT'S WHAT THEY'RE KNOWN FOR. SO WE'RE INVOLVED IN THE LOCAL AREA AND THE REGION AND NATIONALLY; AND IT'S HOW MY WIFE CAME TO CHRIST! SO, IT HAS A SPECIAL PLACE IN OUR HEARTS."
>
> —TODD PETERSON, KICKER FOR THE SEATTLE SEAHAWKS[7]

The even better thing is that we can program to maximize that benefit. Small groups, team-building exercises, community-builder activities, group chores, group skits and team recreational opportunities are all available for use in our relationship tool chest.

When you look at these top two elements according to grade, you'll notice an interesting progression. Seventh graders by far place the highest value on building deeper friendships, with 60 percent choosing this response. As kids who are just entering a new phase of social and academic life, this is understandable.

Eighth-grade students also value highly the prospect of building deeper friendships, but not quite as much as the seventh grade. Forty-two percent of eighth graders chose this option—enough for it to be ranked number one—but that was still 18 percentage points lower than the seventh graders.

Ninth grade is when "more concentrated learning about God" finally surges into the number one spot, with more than half (53%) of students this age selecting that choice. Building deeper friendships is still strongly represented, but only 32 percent of ninth graders chose this— a drop-off of more than 20 percentage points.

Sophomores continue the trend, though not as strongly as the ninth-grade students, with 43 percent of tenth graders choosing more concentrated learning about God as the best thing about camp. By eleventh grade, building deeper friendships begins to reemerge as the highest value, though not completely. Both concentrated learning about God and deeper friendships tie for first, with an equal number of juniors choosing these responses.

Finally, in twelfth grade, the cycle is complete as the seniors, like the junior highers, again rate building deeper friendships as the best thing about a camp or retreat.

> "CAMPS ARE MORE FUN FOR PEOPLE TO MEET NEW PEOPLE FROM OTHER PARTS OF THE COUNTRY, AND FIND OUT THEY'RE MORE ALIKE IN SOME WAYS."
> —NINTH GRADER FROM A REFORMED CHURCH

I think it's no coincidence that the younger kids (junior highers) who are just entering a new relationship setting and the oldest kids (seniors) who are preparing to exit (via graduation) an existing relationship setting are the ones to rate a deepening of friendships highest. There is security in friendships that helps combat some of the insecurity they're facing in other life circumstances.

With that in mind, we'd do well to focus on reaffirming our oldest and youngest group members at camp through more friend-enhancing activities—without ignoring learning, of course. For the middle graders, we certainly don't want to leave out activities that strengthen friendships, but we have a little more freedom to program concentrated learning that we can and should take advantage of at a camp or retreat.

In the survey, the choice which ranked third in response to "the thing I like best" about a camp or retreat was "meeting new people." This choice garnered a healthy 33 percent response rate. That means one out of three students finds the opportunity to expand relational boundaries as the best thing about a camp or retreat.

You can feed that factor by planning plenty of "getting-to-know-you" kinds of crowdbreakers and also by joining with other churches to put on a larger camp or retreat. (That, of course, can also help defray your teenagers' costs for attending the retreat or camp as well!)

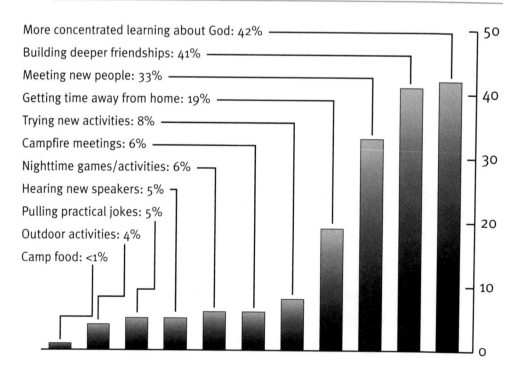

"THE THING I LIKE BEST ABOUT A CAMP OR RETREAT . . ."

More concentrated learning about God: 42%

Building deeper friendships: 41%

Meeting new people: 33%

Getting time away from home: 19%

Trying new activities: 8%

Campfire meetings: 6%

Nighttime games/activities: 6%

Hearing new speakers: 5%

Pulling practical jokes: 5%

Outdoor activities: 4%

Camp food: <1%

WHAT TEENAGERS LIKE BEST AND LEAST ABOUT A CAMP OR RETREAT, BY GRADE:

	LIKE BEST		LIKE LEAST	
7th Grade	Building deeper friendships	60%	(tie) Camp food/Hearing new speakers/Outdoor activities	0%
8th Grade	Building deeper friendships	42%	Camp food	0%
9th Grade	More concentrated learning about God	53%	Camp food	0%
10th Grade	More concentrated learning about God	43%	Camp food	0%
11th Grade	More concentrated learning about God/Building deeper friendships	39%	Camp food	0%
12th Grade	Building deeper friendships	42%	Camp food	2%

Camp Food and Other Disgusting Things

Any exploration of what teenagers like best about camps and retreats is incomplete without a brief look at what kids dislike about these experiences as well.

Top of the "worst" list? Without a question, it's camp food. (Surprised?)

As a teenager, I was spoiled when I went to camp. We had one phenomenal lady who always volunteered to coordinate the food for our camps. Her name then was Kathy Coss, and not only did she love us kids, she loved to cook. In fact, she liked it so much that she ran her own restaurant in a nearby town!

"A RETREAT SHOULD NOT BE SOMETHING THAT HAPPENS JUST BECAUSE IT HAS HAPPENED BEFORE. BEN FRANKLIN SAID, 'LIVING WITHOUT A GOAL IS LIKE SHOOTING WITHOUT A TARGET.' A RETREAT MUST HAVE A PURPOSE. AND THAT PURPOSE SHOULD BE CAREFULLY DEFINED."

—JOHN PEARSON[8]

We *loved* eating camp food she prepared because it was like going out to a nice restaurant every meal! (She told me years later that even with that high-quality cooking, her costs were often less than what other churches spent on below-average meals for their kids.)

> "EARTH'S CRAMMED WITH HEAVEN,
> AND EVERY COMMON
> BUSH AFIRE WITH GOD.
> ONLY HE WHO SEES TAKES
> OFF HIS SHOES,
> THE REST SIT ROUND AND PLUCK
> BLACKBERRIES."
>
> —ELIZABETH BARRETT BROWNING[9]

Then I grew up and entered youth ministry myself. I was in for a rude surprise. I finally found out what other people had been complaining about all along—camp food stinks!

I remember once trying to eat this purple paste that some cook claimed was simply peanut butter and jelly mixed together. (I sneaked my kids out of camp to McDonald's for that meal!) Another time, a cook mixed several boxes of Kraft® macaroni and cheese with a dozen cans of a differently flavored mac-n-cheese and ended up with an awful tasting macaroni-ish mush. (We talked about the value of fasting that night in our discussion group.)

Unfortunately, it appears your teenagers are having the same kind of experience when it comes to camp food. Out of 403 students surveyed, only *two* brave seniors used one of their two choices to pick camp food as one of the best things about these kinds of trips! (Perhaps they have a cook like the one I grew up with!) That's less than one percent of all students surveyed.

Those numbers are pathetic. Think about it—meals are the most frequent program activity of any camp or retreat. Shouldn't *somebody* enjoy them? Hospital food rates higher than camp food! I'm not suggesting we should serve gourmet meals at our camps, but I'm confident we can do better than we have been doing.

When you have guests to your house for a meal, do you slap down a can of chili and a can opener and say, "Have at it!"? Of course not. You do your best to prepare a meal your guests will like enough to be willing to come back.

We need to consider our teenagers as our "guests" at camp and offer them the same courtesy we would at our homes. When we make a sincere effort to upgrade the quality of food at our camps and retreats, we communicate to our students that they are valued and that they deserve at least a decent-tasting and healthy meal when they're in our care. (And we'll enjoy eating at camp a little more ourselves!)

There are a few other low-rated elements that are worth noting here. Outdoor activities, practical jokes and hearing new speakers are a low drawing card for our students. I'm a little surprised that outdoor activities rated so lowly, but I can't argue with the results. Perhaps when it comes to this element of camp, we'd be wise to make outdoor activities available to teens but also to make them optional instead of required.

As far as practical jokes go, my own experience has been that the youth leaders like them more than the teenagers themselves. This survey bears that out as well, with a minority coming to camp in order to play a hoax.

Generally speaking, that means if you've got twenty kids on a retreat, only one will have a great desire to pull a prank. The other nineteen could either care less or would be against it. Is it really worth potentially ruining those nineteen kids' camping experience so that one youth can have a little fun at others' expense? I don't think so.

Speakers are a flashy drawing card among adults, but apparently our teenagers aren't so impressed by the opportunity to hear someone new. Again, only one in twenty is really looking forward to that.

Congratulations! That means they must be getting enough out of your regular youth talks that anything else seems merely ho-hum. (How was that for a little ego-boost?)

Financial Planning

Now before we wrap up this chapter, let's get down to the nitty gritty about camps: the cost.

How much is too much for our students (and their parents)? For what portion of our youth group will our camps be affordable? Obviously the most accurate answer to that will depend on your community, but we can project some starting points based on this survey that should be close to a national average.

Ideally, teenagers would like a camp that costs them each $200 or less. In that situation, the camp appears affordable for a whopping 87 percent (or nearly nine of ten) students involved in our youth groups.

If your camp budget just can't cover expenses by charging students that amount, your next best bet would be a camp that falls in the category of $300 or less per camper. Although that causes about a quarter of your students to drop out, it still should make camp available to a solid majority of your kids (60%).

Generally speaking, to go any higher than $300 per student for a camp is a waste of time (unless you've got a few wealthy members of the congregation willing to donate cash to help defray costs!). Once you ask kids to pay more than $300 for a week-long camping experience, you effectively eliminate about three-fourths of your youth group.

Although the $200 or less and $300 or less price points are good benchmarks, it's worth noting how those figures change according to region and according to gender.

With 94 percent saying they'd pay up to $200 per camper, students from the central and southern regions show the least resistance to that price range. When the camp costs a teenager up to $300, however, kids in this region drop back in line with students from the eastern and midwestern regions, with both groups leveling off at 65 percent (or about two-thirds of potential campers).

The regions that showed the most dramatic resistance to higher pricing were the west and southwest. Only about three-fourths (77%) say they'd pay up to $200 for a camp—well below the national average. If you ask them to pay up to $300 per camper, there's downright rebellion! Only 43 percent of western and southwestern teenagers say they'd pay that much, making them the only sub-population with a majority of students holding that opinion.

The implications are obvious. If you're a youth pastor in California, Texas or another state in the west, realize you must work on a tighter budget and do all you can to keep camp fees at $200 or less.

In terms of guys and girls, it appears that our young men are more the tightwads when it comes to paying for camp. In both categories (up to $200 and up to $300), more girls were willing to pay than guys. Though the difference was marginal with the lower-cost option, it became more pronounced with the higher-cost choice.

Because these guys and girls came from the same regions, the same churches and presumably similar socio-economic backgrounds, I'm honestly mystified at the difference in price resistance. Perhaps girls, who are often characterized as more relationship-oriented, simply value the relational opportunities at a camp more than guys do. Whatever the reason, be aware that this difference exists and plan accordingly. If you're having a "guys-only" trip, you might want to be more sensitive to the cost than you might need to be for a similar "girls-only" trip.

Still, no matter what camp you take your teenagers to, it looks like the best price point across the board is going to be $200 or less per camper. And with it comes the opportunity to impact eternity one life-changing decision at a time.

"WHAT'S THE MAXIMUM AMOUNT YOU'D PAY FOR A ONE-WEEK CAMPING EXPERIENCE WITH YOUR YOUTH GROUP?"

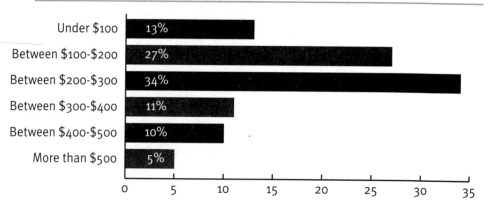

	Willing to pay up to $200	Willing to pay up to $300
PERCENT OF TEENAGERS WILLING TO PAY UP TO $300 FOR A ONE-WEEK CAMP, BY REGION AND GENDER		
Eastern and Midwestern Regions	89%	65%
Central and Southern Regions	94%	65%
Southwestern and Western Regions	77%	43%
Males	86%	56%
Females	88%	63%

Chapter Summary and Observations

For an overwhelming majority of our teenagers, life-changing decisions happen at camp.

That's so exciting! We're doing something right! For some reason, God has chosen to bless our efforts at camps and retreats by giving us an inordinate amount of positive decisions that happen at these locations.

Our responsibility, then, is twofold: 1) Take time to regularly thank God for being involved in these experiences and ask him to continue that involvement, and 2) be diligent to prepare and plan for the highest-quality camping experience we can realistically provide the teenagers in our care.

Teenagers like to learn about God and build deeper friendships at camps and retreats. And, unfortunately, camp food still stinks.

This news is a dream for those of us who do our own programming for our camps. Now that we know what students like best in our camps and retreats, we can program to fuel that interest in God and relationships. Thankfully, there are hundreds of quality resources for youth ministry to help you do that. Check your local Christian bookstore to find materials best suited for your youth group.

If the camp your group attends handles the programming aspects for you, be sure to voice to the camp directors your concerns about the program. Emphasize to them that you think two primary purposes of the camp should be to build deeper friendships and to provide more concentrated time for learning about God. (Feel free to show them a copy of this book to support your argument!) Then ask them to program accordingly and offer to assist them if they would like that.

As far as the camp food goes, do your best to change this negative perception about meals and you'll win friends for life.

The best price for a camp is $200 or less per camper. When camp costs go over $300, most kids can't go.

Although many parents still help their kids pay for camp, we've got to remember that growing numbers of our teenagers must pay at least a portion of these expenses themselves. For people who earn their money working at the mall on weekends or at McDonald's before and after school, that can be a challenge. You always appreciate buying something that's comfortable for your budget, so do your students a favor and work hard to make your camps something that is comfortable for their budgets as well.

If there's just no way you can put on a camp for less than $300 per person, consider replacing camp with an extended weekend retreat. Try a Friday through Monday trip with a smaller budget than a full-fledged camp. Or you might become a fund-raising fanatic for your teenagers, soliciting donations from church members and sympathetic businesses in your community.

Whatever you do, remember that money alone is an awfully poor reason for a teen in your youth group to have to stay home instead of go to camp. But if your camp costs too much, that may be exactly the reason why some of your kids miss out.

For Personal Reflection

Take a few moments now to process your own reaction to the information in this chapter. Use these questions to help spark your thinking:

- *What life-changing decisions have you seen happen at a camp or retreat? What ones do you hope to see happen at your next camp/retreat?*

- *How would you define "learning about God" and "deepening friendships"? How do you recognize when it happens? What can you do to facilitate those things happening at your camps and retreats?*

- *Look at the budget for your last camp or retreat. Where could you cut costs? Which areas deserve more money? How can you creatively divide up $200 (or less) per person for expenses and still avoid having to serve peanut butter paste for lunch?*

> "EACH ONE SHOULD USE WHATEVER GIFT HE HAS
> RECEIVED TO SERVE OTHERS, FAITHFULLY
> ADMINISTERING GOD'S GRACE IN ITS
> VARIOUS FORMS."
> —1 PETER 4:10

Chapter 8

WHAT I WISH MY YOUTH LEADER KNEW ABOUT . . .

SERVICE AND MISSION PROJECTS

Not long ago, a young boy discovered the powerful ministry of Mother Teresa. From the safety of his home in America, he learned how this little woman with great faith reached out to the sick and dying of Calcutta, India. He was moved to hear she had dedicated her life to "the poorest of the poor" and inspired by the way that simple dedication of service had literally changed the world.

> "SERVICE APPEARS TO BE MORE POWERFUL IN NURTURING FAITH THAN IS SUNDAY SCHOOL, BIBLE STUDY, OR PARTICIPATION IN WORSHIP. THIS IS TRUE BECAUSE, AS FAYE CASKEY, A RELIGIOUS EDUCATOR WITH EXPERIENCE IN SERVICE-LEARNING, SAYS, 'WE BEHAVE OURSELVES INTO THINKING AND FEELING MORE QUICKLY THAN WE FEEL OURSELVES INTO BEHAVING.'"
>
> —PETER L. BENSON AND EUGENE C. ROEHLKEPARTAIN[1]

Before Mother Teresa died in 1997, that boy sent her a letter explaining how much he admired her work and asking for advice. "How can I make a difference with my life like you have with yours in Calcutta?" he queried. Then he waited for a response.

Weeks passed, then months. Just about the time he was ready to give up, a letter arrived with a postmark from Calcutta, India. Excitedly the boy tore open the envelope. Finally he would learn the secret of how to make a difference with his life!

The reply from Mother Teresa was merely four words, but those four words changed that boy's life and mission. Here's what she said:

"Find your own Calcutta."

So he did.[2]

Mother Teresa's advice is as timeless as the mission of service on which she spent her life. And it's advice we can both share with our teenagers and use to help our teenagers impact others through their service on youth group service and mission trips.

The benefits of this kind of activity are unparalleled. In their landmark book, *Beyond Leaf Raking*, Peter L. Benson and Eugene Roehlkepartain of the Search Institute document the following benefits of youth being involved in service opportunities:[3]

- It "bonds" youth to the church, deepening loyalty to a specific congregation.

- It nurtures young people's growth in faith.

- It gives young people new skills and perspectives.

- It "emphasizes intergenerational contact" and "creates a sense of community in which people help one another develop faith and values."

- It "encourages independent thinking and questioning."

- It "provides a positive climate where young people are influenced positively by their peers."

- It "promotes healthy lifestyles and choices among teenagers."

- It increases the likelihood that teenagers will grow up to be adults who are involved in service and justice.

- In a youth group, it provides a shared task and purpose, facilitates increased interdependence, enriches study, trains young leaders and creates new relationships.

- In a community, it empowers recipients of service to regain control of their lives, mobilizes teenagers as community "activists" and changes teenagers' perception in the eyes of adults in positive ways.

The list goes on and on! I could continue for several pages, but I believe the point is made: Including teenagers in service is good for everyone involved. That's good news for us, because Benson and Roehlkepartain report that "the church tends to be the main gateway to service for teenagers."[4]

But how effective are we in providing the kind of service and mission opportunities our teens really desire? I asked a few questions on my survey that were designed to discover a) where teenagers want to serve; b) how often they want to serve; and c) what factors influence their decision of whether or not to participate in service.

Here's what I found out.

Location, Location, Location

America's teenagers today are generally considered to be more interested in changing the world

"I FEEL HAPPY AND PROUD OF MYSELF BECAUSE I HELPED SOMEBODY ELSE INSTEAD OF MYSELF."

—TENTH-GRADE FEMALE FROM TEXAS AFTER COMPLETING A SERVICE PROJECT/MISSION TRIP next door than they are in changing the world at large. What we didn't know is that "next door" is a little farther away than we thought.

I gave students a choice of joining a service/mission project somewhere outside the U.S., somewhere outside their home state but still within the U.S., somewhere within their home state or right in their own community. The easy winner was somewhere outside the home state but within the U.S. Nearly half of all students (48%) chose this option. (This might not be too surprising since those taking the survey were participating in a Reach Workcamp within the U.S.)

It seems our teenagers have a little wanderlust after all. Combining service with travel, then, just heightens the appeal of reaching out to others. The only trouble with this statistic is that we as youth leaders seem to have overestimated the amount of travel our kids really want!

When you compare the results of my survey with teens with the results of the smaller survey with youth leaders, there are some noticeable discrepancies. For starters, although about half of teenagers said they wanted to travel within the United States for a service/mission project, only one in five of the youth leaders felt that was what teenagers would choose. Youth leaders instead voted heavily in favor of a teen desire to travel abroad—something teenagers themselves rated as much less important.

> "SEVERAL YEARS AGO I GOT TO GO TO ASIA FOR THE SUMMER. IT WAS A GREAT OPPORTUNITY FOR ME TO SEE CHRISTIANITY FROM A NON-TWENTIETH-CENTURY AMERICAN SLANT. WHAT THAT DID FOR ME WAS CONFIRMED THE TRUTH OF THE ESSENCE OF CHRISTIANITY, AND IT CHALLENGED MY SOMEWHAT RIGID AND POSSIBLY MISINFORMED OPINIONS ABOUT PERIPHERAL ISSUES. . . . MANY OF THE EXPERIENCES I HAD THERE WITH PEOPLE WHO HAD A DIFFERENT SLANT REALLY DEEPENED AND BROADENED AND ENRICHED MY VIEW OF WHAT GOD WAS DOING HERE. I WENT, 'WOW, I WANT TO DO THAT AGAIN!'"
>
> —LATE CHRISTIAN MUSIC ARTIST, RICH MULLINS, WHO SPENT THE LAST YEARS OF HIS LIFE LIVING AND TEACHING ON A NAVAJO RESERVATION[5]

Still, it's worth noting that a solid percentage of teenagers are interested in a trip outside U.S. borders. Just under one in three (30%)

students listed that option as his or her number one preference. Taken in conjunction with those who would choose to travel within the U.S., that means nearly four out of every five (78%) students would choose a trip outside their home state as their first preference for where to locate a service or mission project.

When you break those numbers down by region, however, there's an interesting diversity of opinion regarding the most favorable location. Looking at the data as a whole, only 22 percent of youth group members indicated an interest in serving in their own community or state. But watch what happens when each region tallies its votes separately.

In the central and southern regions of the states, a mere 10 percent, or one out of every ten students, is interested in staying close to home for a service or mission project. Perhaps they're tired of their areas, perhaps they're simply more adventurous or they more deeply feel a need to touch the world at large. Whatever the reason, simply having a service or mission project nearby isn't much motivation for these kids to join in.

> "IT'S A GREAT SENSATION KNOWING THAT YOU'RE [SERVING] THE LORD AND THAT YOU'VE HELPED SOMEONE—OR YOURSELF—GROW CLOSER TO GOD!"
>
> —TWELFTH GRADER FROM MISSOURI

If you're a youth pastor in this area, you'll need to take that realization into account when planning opportunities for your group to serve. If you do plan a local or near-local project, make sure it's something good enough to make up for the lack of travel these kids desperately desire.

In the eastern and midwestern regions, teenagers run close to the national average in their desire to stay at home. A respectable one in five (20%) would prefer this option. For you youth pastors in these regions, it's probably safe to assume that although you'd get greater participation by traveling outside state lines, you still probably won't get much opposition to a service/mission project that occasionally lands within those lines.

How about those of you in the southwestern and western regions? Your kids break the curve. A whopping 38 percent, or more than one-third of your group, is determined to change the world by changing their home. That's nearly double the number of kids who feel likewise in the eastern and midwestern regions and more than triple the number of teenagers of similar opinion in the central and southern regions.

> "AFTER A SERVICE PROJECT, I GET A GOOD FEELING, A SENSE OF ACCOM-PLISHMENT. ESPECIALLY THIS YEAR BECAUSE I'VE NEVER DONE ANY-THING LIKE THIS BEFORE WHERE YOU ACTUALLY HELP BUILD STUFF."
>
> —TENTH-GRADE FEMALE FROM FLORIDA

In fact, more teenagers in the southwestern and western regions would rather stay home than would choose either the option to travel outside state borders or outside national borders. That's a little surprising, given that kids in these states have much closer access to Mexico. Still, the implications are clear for those of you ministering in the west and southwest. Serve locally first, globally second.

"WHERE WOULD YOU MOST LIKE FOR YOU AND YOUR YOUTH GROUP TO PARTICIPATE IN A SERVICE/MISSION PROJECT?"

	TEENAGERS' RESPONSES	YOUTH LEADERS' RESPONSES
Somewhere outside your state, but in the U.S.	48%	20%
Somewhere outside the U.S.	30%	50%
Right in your community	13%	20%
Somewhere within your state	9%	5%

PERCENT OF TEENAGERS WHO DESIRE A SERVICE/MISSION PROJECT TO TAKE PLACE WITHIN THEIR OWN COMMUNITY OR STATE, BY REGION

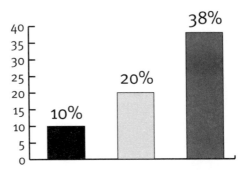

■ Central and Southern Regions

□ Eastern and Midwestern Regions

■ Southwestern and Western Regions

Out of This World?

Let's take a moment now to explore teen attitudes toward international travel in regard to service and mission projects. Looking at the data, I don't think we can characterize either GenX or Millennial Gen teenagers as a generation of hard-core missionaries, but I am encouraged by the solid percentage of teens who are interested in a cross-cultural service experience.

As a total population, a good 30 percent, or three of every ten teenagers, rated an international mission as their favorite choice. Now, that's not enough to warrant a trip to Mexico or Haiti every year, but it is enough to consider doing something like that at least once in each student's middle school or high school experience.

These figures become especially significant when you compare the individual grades. It appears that interest in cross-cultural service opportunities is greatest among the younger classes and declines noticeably as students get older.

Seventh graders are by far the most eager to travel beyond America's borders—perhaps because they haven't experienced a trip like this yet. A full 47 percent—nearly half—of these kids wants to board that plane to nowhere in search of mission opportunities. That could reflect the optimism that characterizes the Millennial Gen thus far or the increasing cultural diversity these younger kids have experienced. Or it could simply be that younger kids have fewer fears of culture shock. Whatever the case, this survey indicates that, based on teens' desire, the ideal time to take kids across the world is during the early middle school years. Dealing with parental desire and support might be an entirely different thing.

A SURVEY OF 4,000 YOUNG PEOPLE BY RESEARCHERS DAN CONRAD AND DIANE HEDIN REVEALED THAT 86 PERCENT OR MORE OF TEENAGERS SAY SERVICE OPPORTUNITIES HELPED THEM GAIN THESE BENEFITS:[6]

- CONCERN FOR FELLOW HUMAN BEINGS
- ABILITY TO GET THINGS DONE AND WORK SMOOTHLY WITH OTHERS
- REALISTIC ATTITUDES TOWARD OTHER PEOPLE
- SELF-MOTIVATION TO LEARN, PARTICIPATE AND ACHIEVE
- CONFIDENCE, COMPETENCE AND SELF-AWARENESS
- RESPONSIBILITY TO THE GROUP
- OPENNESS TO NEW EXPERIENCES
- SENSE OF USEFULNESS IN RELATION TO THE COMMUNITY
- PROBLEM-SOLVING SKILLS
- FEELINGS OF ASSERTIVENESS AND INDEPENDENCE

Eighth and ninth graders show a respectable interest in serving outside the United States, but far fewer of them are interested in it than their counterparts in seventh grade. Still a healthy 35 percent, roughly one in three, would choose to travel beyond America's borders to participate in a service or mission project.

From there, you'll notice a second significant drop-off in interest. A good number of students in tenth and eleventh grades are still interested in international travel, but now the number drops to about one in four (28%). Finally, America's seniors finish the progression with one last slight decline. Only 26 percent of twelfth graders want to cross cultures, the lowest number of any grade represented.

So, it appears our window of opportunity for cross-cultural missions is opened widest when our teenagers are youngest. Typically, however, we tend to reserve those kinds of trips for the upper classes. Perhaps it's time to rethink that strategy and make more international service opportunities available to the younger grades, then gradually decrease the number of opportunities as students get older.

PERCENT OF TEENAGERS WHO DESIRE A SERVICE/MISSION PROJECT TO TAKE PLACE OUTSIDE THE U.S., BY GRADE

	7TH	8TH	9TH	10TH	11TH	12TH
Percentage	47%	35%	35%	28%	28%	26%
Where Ranked by Grade	1	2	2	2	2	2

How Much Is Too Much?

The story of King Midas is a classic parable. The king loves gold. Can't get enough of it. Wishes everything he touched would turn to gold. Alakazaam! He gets his wish. At first he's overjoyed, turning everything he finds into lovely, glittery gold.

Then he realizes his first problem: He can't eat! Whenever food touches his lips, it turns to gold. Next comes the second problem. Without thinking, he reaches to embrace his daughter and turns her into gold as well. Our poor hero is now heartbroken. He's finally discovered there's something to that phrase, "too much of a good thing." (For those of you who are worried, the story has a happy ending. King Midas recants his wish. Everything is restored to normal, and all live happily ever after.)

Service and mission projects are a bit like King Midas's gold. Incorporating these into a youth ministry is a valuable, life-changing practice. But can there be such a thing as too much service for these kids? Let's see what our survey reveals.

The first thing I notice about teenagers' responses on this topic is that our students have a high "tolerance" for, or a strong internal motivation for, service and mission projects. An overwhelming 93 percent recommended that service/mission projects happen in their youth groups on an annual basis—or sooner! This is one area where my sample of youth pastors gauged teen sentiment almost exactly correct. Among the youth leaders, 95 percent made the same recommendation.

If you need to be more specific about when to schedule service and mission projects, students strongly supported the idea of holding these events "once or twice a year." Nearly two-thirds of those teenagers surveyed chose this response, making it the number one choice.

The next closest choice wasn't really close at all. "At least once a month" ranked number two among teenagers, but at 30 percent it garnered less than half the number of respondents that the top-ranked choice got. Still, 30 percent is nothing to sneeze at. Imagine how a 30 percent raise might positively affect your family's income and you realize this is still a significant number of teenagers interested in frequent service opportunities.

Once you get past the first two choices of teenagers, the rest are barely worth mentioning. None of the other options ("once every two years," "once every three years," "once every four years" and "never") got so much as five percent recognition. This is especially apparent when you consider that among twelfth graders, 98 percent chose one of the top two responses, and only 2 percent selected any of the other four options.

"WE JUST GOT OFF A SERVICE PROJECT—A CANNED FOOD DRIVE. IT WAS EXCITING TO GET BACK AND TELL OUR GROUP ABOUT THE EXPERIENCE! IT'S FUN TO TALK ABOUT IT AND ENCOURAGE THEM TO DO IT WITH US THE NEXT TIME."

—NINTH-GRADE MALE FROM A CHARISMATIC CHURCH

Suffice it to say, then, if you wait more than a year to give your teens a formal opportunity to serve, you do both them and God a great disservice.

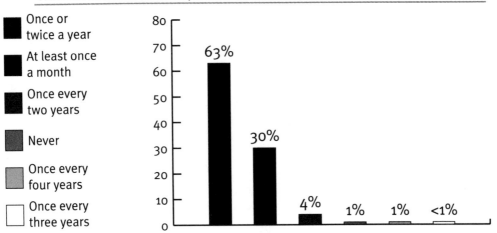

"How often do you think you and your youth group should participate in a service/mission project?"

- ■ Once or twice a year
- ■ At least once a month
- ■ Once every two years
- ■ Never
- ■ Once every four years
- ☐ Once every three years

63% 30% 4% 1% 1% <1%

Deciding Factors

Having settled the location and frequency of service/mission projects, I felt it was important to know what factors teens considered most vital when deciding whether or not to participate. I gave kids eight factors to choose from and asked them to rate which was the most important. I asked youth leaders to do the same and then compared the results.

First the bad news. Generally speaking, we youth leaders are out of touch with the importance our teenagers place on the price tag associated with events such as these. Youth leaders ranked "the cost" in a weak tie for fourth among the factors that kids consider most important. Teenagers, on the other hand, ranked "the cost" at number one. Due to rounding, "the cost" tied for first place, but I think it's important for you to know that this choice did indeed receive the highest number of individual votes among teenagers.

> "After the Reach Workcamp, I felt a big sense of accomplishment and good about myself for doing things for other people. [And I felt] good that there are things like this going on."
>
> —Ninth-grade male from Pennsylvania

Youth leaders, take note: We must be diligent to structure our service and mission projects in such a way as to make them financially feasible for our teenagers and their families. When we ignore the great influence dollars and cents have on our students' ability to participate, we ignore potential opportunities to impact the kingdom of God in our teenagers. Taking a lesson from the previous chapter, I'd recommend we limit the cost of these kinds of projects to $300 or less per student. (That means you'll need to participate in some creative fund-raising in order to take your group overseas.)

> "WE STILL LIVE WITH OVER A BILLION DESPERATELY POOR NEIGHBORS. ANOTHER TWO BILLION STRUGGLE IN NEAR POVERTY WITH VERY LITTLE HOPE FOR A DECENT LIFE. NOR HAS GOD'S SPECIAL CONCERN FOR THE POOR CHANGED. HUNDREDS OF BIBLICAL TEXTS TELL US THAT GOD STILL MEASURES OUR SOCIETIES BY WHAT WE DO TO THE POOREST."
>
> —RONALD J. SIDER[7]

Now for the good news. The other two areas youth group members rated as important deciding factors are ones that youth leaders gave an equally strong importance rating. About one in five students (21%) is very concerned about the "type of work" they'll do while serving—something that's a valid concern.

Several years ago I took a group of junior highers to San Francisco to work on the grounds of an inner-city Christian school. When we arrived, we saw a school that was overrun with weeds and debris, had broken equipment and needed some minor, but important, structural repairs. The kids were excited—here they were going to make a difference and be able to see that difference take shape.

Except that the coordinator at the school didn't want youngsters doing construction and didn't really expect my junior highers to be able to accomplish much. He set one group of guys to carrying branches from one place to another, and the rest of us were to tackle the basketball court, cleaning out the weeds that had grown through the cracks in the pavement.

Although the cracks in the pavement were numerous, we had that court cleaned and ready to be filled with asphalt in about two hours. When we asked for the asphalt, the school official looked surprised. Had we already finished the cleaning? He didn't have but one small bucket of asphalt—enough to fill barely one-tenth of the cracks on the court—and wasn't going to be getting more anytime soon. He all but admitted he'd simply given us "busywork" to pass the day.

You should have seen the look on those kids' faces. They felt betrayed and useless. They knew that without filling the holes, those weeds would grow back in a week's time. They'd wasted their labor doing meaningless work for a man who expected less than nothing from them because they were young.

Due to the coordinator's lack of belief in the students, that week was probably the worst "service" project in which I've involved my teenagers. My kids knew none of the projects they were assigned to do had any lasting impact and decided to give only their very least.

Our teenagers want to know they're doing something worthwhile, so they rate "the type of work" as one of the highest factors that influences their decisions. Be careful to choose work that's worthy of the laborer—we've got enough cracked basketball courts without cracking a youth's heart for service too.

The third factor that teens use to determine whether or not to participate in a service or mission project is whether or not their friends are going. Twenty-one percent of those surveyed listed this option.

Did I mention these young people value relationships? I think so—about every chapter! I don't mean to be a broken record, but that element kept coming up throughout the survey! We'd be wise to take notice.

Two lower-rated items still scored respectably and are worth mentioning. The Bible's encouragement to serve was enough reason for 16 percent of teenagers to participate in a service or mission project. For these kids—and for the others who might not be aware of it—we need to bring to the fore how our projects fulfill that encouragement from Scripture.

And, of course, about 10 percent of our students just wanna have fun—and that's OK. A job well done is ample reason to celebrate, so if possible, plan at least one opportunity for teens just to play after completing a service.

It's important to note here, too, that one other factor that wasn't included on the survey still got a lot of write-in responses. The scheduling of a service/mission project seemed a primary concern to quite a few teens.

This was the only time in the survey a significant number of young people wrote in an all-new, yet similar, response to a question. In the busy life of a teenager, knowing exactly when a service/mission is planned seemed an important factor. My guess is that had I thought to include "Time Schedule" as one of the options, this choice would have ranked up with the top three finishers.

Surprisingly, things such as the specific location, safety issues and housing matter very little to teenagers intent on serving. My hunch is they want to go where the need is—wherever that may be. Once there, they pretty much trust their leaders (you!) to look out for their safety and to be prepared for potential accidents. And they're more concerned about accomplishing their task than about sleeping in a comfy bed.

What great attitudes! These numbers show that, for the most part, our teenagers really have their hearts in the right place when it comes to serving others. We are privileged to be able to serve alongside them. Let's always remember that.

DECIDING FACTORS FOR INVOLVEMENT IN A YOUTH GROUP
SERVICE OR MISSION PROJECT

	TEENAGERS' RESPONSES	YOUTH LEADERS' RESPONSES
The cost	21%	5%
The type of work we'll do	21%	35%
Which of my friends are going	21%	40%
The Bible's encouragement to serve	16%	0%
Whether or not fun activities are included	10%	5%
The location	4%	10%
Safety issues	4%	0%
The accommodations	2%	0%

Chapter Summary and Observations

When it comes to service and mission projects, teenagers love to travel.

Break out your maps, boys and girls, it's time to hit the open road!

Look for opportunities to take your kids outside your state, and you've already won nearly 80 percent of those group members to your cause. Check denominational "cousin churches" to find those opportunities. Or take your students to a service/mission experience coordinated by another organization such as Reach Workcamps, Group Workcamps or The Center for Student Ministries.

The only exception to this rule could be for youth pastors in the West and Southwest. Remember, your teenagers will often prefer something nearer, within state lines. Still, you might want to ask them. Perhaps this year they'll want to stay home and next year they'll want to travel.

And speaking of travel, don't rule out international travel unless it's simply not feasible. You won't get your entire youth group to go, but a solid core of kids—particularly those in middle school—can and will make that a worthwhile experience.

Teenagers don't want to wait too long between service/mission projects.

What a great discovery! We've got teenagers who can't wait to get their hands dirty on behalf of someone in need. Take advantage of that now—you may not always have teens who are self-motivated to participate like this.

Generally speaking, you'll want to program for at least one service or mission project on an annual basis, though many students are willing to do more, up to at least once a month. My suggestion would be to plan one big mission trip each year (such as a Reach Workcamp or an international expedition) and then several monthly or bimonthly smaller projects in your community throughout the year.

Cost, type of work and friends are the primary factors that influence whether or not a teenager participates in a service/mission project.

The rules are simple here:

• Keep the prices down.

• Make the work meaningful.

• Encourage groups of friends to go.

Follow those guidelines and you've already helped about two-thirds of your teenagers decide in favor of the trip.

So what are you waiting for? Get those sign-up sheets ready tonight!

For Personal Reflection

Take a few moments now to process your own reaction to the information in this chapter. Use these questions to help spark your thinking:

- *What went through your mind as you read the survey results in this chapter?*

- *What are five specific service or mission projects you think would be appropriate for your youth group? How can you use what you've learned in this chapter to maximize those service experiences for teenagers?*

- *What are your favorite memories from past service and mission projects with teenagers? Why not take a moment now to thank God for the privilege of experiencing those moments with teens?*

Chapter 9

WHAT I WISH MY YOUTH LEADER KNEW ABOUT . . .

SPECIAL EVENTS

We advertised it as "A Day with Audio Adrenaline!" This premiere Christian band was coming in concert to our area, and our youth group was going as a special event. As an added bonus, three lucky high schoolers who won a drawing would get to accompany me to the concert venue early in the day to interview and "hang out" with the band.

The day came for the interview, and all the members of AudioA were great. They chatted casually with my teenagers as if they'd been friends for life. Ben Cissell, the drummer, took the kids on a tour of the venue. The road manager for the band made the kids "honorary roadies" and put them to work setting up equipment. Lead singer, Mark Stuart, serenaded us with wacky, made-up lyrics during the sound check. All in all things were going well.

Then the concert doors opened to the public and the rest of our youth group arrived for the show. By now, the band members were locked away in their dressing rooms, getting ready to perform. The three lucky teenagers and I went to find our seats. We were on the sound board platform—great seats!

> A TEEN'S ADVICE FOR YOUTH LEADERS: "GET A LOT MORE YOUTH INVOLVED. THE MORE KIDS THERE ARE, THE MORE FUN IT IS. DO MORE TRIPS, CONCERTS, [AND] FUN STUFF OTHER THAN MEETINGS IN THE CHURCH BASEMENT."
>
> —NINTH-GRADE MALE FROM PENNSYLVANIA

The rest of the youth group, however, was not so fortunate. Turns out the group tickets we'd bought were on the dead-last, can't-get-any-further-away-without-moving-to-Alaska row of the 7,000 seat arena! Our teens were bummed but still excited for the show.

When Ben Cissell found out what had happened, he just grinned, saying, "Hey, let's go see them!" Even though he was due on stage in fifteen minutes, he sneaked through the gathering crowd, hiked all the way up to the nosebleed section and introduced himself to the twenty or so kids who had come. He took time to shake hands, sign a few autographs, shoot the breeze and simply be available to my kids. Then, with barely minutes to spare, he went back up front and joined the band in rocking the house.

"WHEN WE FIRST STARTED, OUR GOAL WAS TO BE IN MISSIONS, TO BE EVANGELICAL, AND TO BE A MINISTRY. DURING THE FIRST COUPLE OF YEARS I THOUGHT IT WAS. BUT IT REALLY WASN'T UNTIL JUST RECENTLY THAT WE'VE BEGUN SEEING THE EFFECTS OF THAT MINISTRY. LIKE WHEN WE TRAVEL AROUND THE COUNTRY AND WE COME BACK TO A CITY THAT WE'VE BEEN TO BEFORE AND KIDS WILL COME UP AND SAY, 'I CAME TO YOUR SHOW WHEN YOU GUYS WERE HERE LAST YEAR. THIS IS MY FRIEND, HE CAME AND WASN'T A CHRISTIAN, BUT NOW HE'S A CHRISTIAN.' . . . EVERY NIGHT WE PROBABLY MEET A COUPLE OF KIDS THAT SAY THAT TO US."

—BOB HERDMAN OF AUDIO ADRENALINE[1]

Needless to say, Audio Adrenaline is now one of the youth group favorites in my church! It's been nearly two years since that concert, but kids still talk about the fun they had meeting AudioA's drummer and rockin' out in the back row. A youth group memory was made, all because we scheduled a special event.

Personally, I think that these kinds of special events are one of the more enjoyable things about being involved in ministry to youth. Think about it. Our "work" consists of trips to amusement parks, swim parties, beach trips, pizza nights, sporting events and more. Now, I know that being in charge of those kinds of events can be stressful, but it still beats most other kinds of work.

I remember when I was on staff at a church in southern California, part of my job was to coordinate a trip to the beach every Monday of summer. For some rea-son, my wife—who worked the 9-to-5 job that earned most of our family income—never saw the added sunburn risk as much of a job hazard for me!

Still, there are times when a special event just flops royally. (Like the time I put on a dance, and only three kids showed up!) So it's important to know things such as what types of events our teenagers like, how much our group members are willing to pay for an event and whether or not kids are using these events as evangelistic tools for reaching their friends. Let's discover what teenagers had to say about those things.

So, Whaddya Wanna Do This Weekend?

Gathering input from other youth leaders, I made a list of sixteen special event categories that are typical in a youth ministry. Then I asked survey respondents to mark their top two choices to reveal which special events they most liked to see in their home youth groups. The result was an amazing display of diversity, with four or five spe-cific categories that pulled away from the pack to land in the top spots.

> INTERVIEWER: "WHY DO YOU AND YOUR FRIENDS ATTEND SPECIAL YOUTH GROUP EVENTS?"
> NINTH GRADER FROM INDIANA: "JUST TO GET TOGETHER IN A CHRISTIAN ATMOSPHERE. IT'S LOTS OF FUN, BUT [WE GO] MOSTLY FOR THE ATMOSPHERE THAT'S GOING AROUND. I FEEL REALLY COMFORTABLE THERE."

If special events were football teams, the post-season might look like this:

Lock-ins and Christian Music Concerts would go head-to-head in a battle for the Super Bowl Championship.

Amusement Parks and Snow Skiing would barely miss the champi-onship game, losing perhaps by a field goal to Lock-ins and Christian Music Concerts.

Other playoff teams would include Hiking/Outdoor Activities, Youth Rallies and Beach Parties. And the occasional underdog who might squeak into the post-season would be Movie Nights or Pizza Nights.

What a great variety of interest among our teenagers! It looks like just about anything we do will be met with enthusiasm from a good number of our youth. Also, it's worth noting that although a variety of interests showed up, lock-ins and Christian music concerts dominated the rankings—even among the older grades.

I honestly had expected lock-ins to fare well among middle schoolers and then drop in the rankings as students got older. That just wasn't the case. The upper classes supported lock-ins more often than the lower classes, with sophomores, juniors and seniors all ranking lock-ins in their grades' number one spot.

> "WHEN I DO A CONCERT, OFTEN I LIKE TO START THE EVENING BY LETTING PEOPLE KNOW MY PURPOSE— THAT I HOPE IT WILL BE A WORSHIP EXPERIENCE, NOT JUST A SHOW. I WANT IT TO BE AN ENCOURAGEMENT TO ALL OF US TO STAND STRONG FOR GOD AND TO LIVE A RADICAL CHRISTIAN LIFE, SUPPORTING EACH OTHER AND RELYING ON HIM."
> —REBECCA ST. JAMES[2]

Contemporary Christian music (CCM) is also a big draw among our teenagers, coming very close to matching lock-ins in appeal. Like lock-ins, CCM concerts appeared in the top three no matter how the data broke down. In fact, CCM concerts even broke lock-ins' stranglehold on the top spot in the southwestern and western regions, narrowly coming in at number one for the kids in those areas.

Though not as strong as lock-ins or CCM concerts, other heavyweight choices for special events were amusement parks and snow skiing. Amusement parks ranked in the top four in every region of the United States and also beat out both lock-ins and CCM concerts among the eighth graders in this survey.

Snow skiing's strong showing is something of a surprise, simply because it's perceived as primarily a regional sport. For example, where do you ski in Florida? Still, this option ranked in the top five of the overall totals and in the top five among each region represented.

Hiking/outdoor activities and beach parties also had a respectable following among teenagers. Beyond that is a potpourri of special events (youth rallies, pizza nights, movie nights, swim parties and so on) that garners limited support from generally equal numbers of teenagers.

ACCORDING TO THE AMUSEMENT PARK INDUSTRY, OVER 280 MILLION PEOPLE—A FULL 30 MILLION MORE THAN OUR NATIONAL POPULATION—VISIT AMUSEMENT PARKS LOCATED IN THE UNITED STATES EACH YEAR.[3]

The overall picture, then? This portion of the survey tells me that even though some events are more strongly favored than others, we've got a lot of freedom to create special events for our groups. With that in mind, we might as well take to heart the old Pepsi slogan: "Be Young. Have Fun." (But do it in youth group!)

"WHICH TYPES OF SPECIAL EVENTS DO YOU LIKE TO SEE IN YOUR YOUTH GROUP?" (CIRCLE UP TO TWO.)

Event	Percentage
Lock-ins	37%
Christian music concerts	29%
Amusement parks	16%
Snow skiing	14%
Hiking/outdoor activities	10%
Beach parties	10%
Youth rallies	8%
Pizza nights	7%
Movie nights	6%
Swim parties	6%
Game nights	5%
Spectator sporting events	4%
Hayrides	4%
Picnics	3%
Water skiing	3%
Skate parties	1%

TEENAGERS' TOP FIVE CHOICES FOR SPECIAL EVENTS

	7TH	8TH	9TH	10TH	11TH	12TH
BY GRADE:						
Lock-ins	47%	29%	26%	42%	51%	28%
Amusement parks	40%	33%	16%	—	10%	18%
Christian music concerts	27%	29%	32%	34%	23%	25%
Snow skiing	20%	17%	16%	—	13%	20%
Movie nights	20%	13%	—	—	—	—
Youth rallies	—	13%	—	12%	—	—
Hiking/outdoor activities	—	13%	—	11%	14%	—
Beach parties	—	—	15%	—	—	16%
Pizza nights	—	—	—	11%	—	—

	EASTERN/MIDWESTERN	CENTRAL/SOUTHERN	SOUTHWESTERN/WESTERN
BY REGION:			
Lock-ins	36%	48%	29%
Amusement parks	16%	14%	19%
Christian music concerts	29%	25%	30%
Snow skiing	16%	14%	11%
Movie nights	—	—	—
Youth rallies	—	—	11%
Hiking/outdoor activities	11%	14%	—
Beach parties	—	16%	—
Pizza nights	—	—	—

What's Your Price Range?

Few things in life are free—including most youth group special events. So when you're planning your next lock-in, concert, ski day or amusement park trip, what kind of budget will your kids find affordable?

Looking at the national average, it seems that: 1) teenagers aren't as cheap as we sometimes assume, and 2) they don't have as much disposable income as we sometimes assume either.

According to the students in this survey, virtually everyone can afford to pay $5 or less for a youth group event. An astounding 99 percent of teenagers didn't blink an eye at that cost. Additionally, nearly everyone can afford an event that runs up to $10. More than nine of ten students (92%) say that amount is affordable for them.

Those numbers are good news for organizers of lock-ins, some CCM concerts, movie nights, pizza parties and the like. It means that even on a limited budget we can still provide youth group events that our teenagers enjoy—and can afford.

FROM A CARTOON BY JOHN MCPHERSON: "TO KEEP THE KIDS FROM GETTING OUT? ARE YOU KIDDING? WE LOCK IT UP TO KEEP THE *TEACHERS* FROM GETTING OUT!"[4]

When we move up to some of the moderately expensive events such as youth rallies, baseball games and concerts with more well-known Christian artists, we begin to see a drop-off in participation. At roughly $20 per person, these kinds of activities cause more than one out of four students (26%) to get left behind.

The biggest drop-off, however, happens at the $30 price point. When a ski day, amusement park, professional football game or big-name CCM concert hits or exceeds this price point, it effectively eliminates more than half (57%) of the youth group. They simply can't afford to pay the few extra dollars required to participate.

Surprisingly, the affordability of these three price points affects youth in each region of the U.S. in very similar ways. Regardless of the region, about nine in ten students still say they can afford an event that costs $10 or less. At the $20 cutoff, you still have about three-fourths of teenagers in each region who say they can pay that amount.

The biggest regional differences show up in the $30 price range. Here the central and southern regions still maintain a majority of students who say they'll part with the money for the event. No other region or sub-population studied held a majority at that price point. That includes males, females and students from each individual grade.

The southwestern and western regions again showed the strongest resistance to inflated prices. With a cost of $30, seven of ten students (70%) in this region report that the youth group event becomes unaffordable.

The data seems to indicate, then, that we'd be wise to schedule low-to moderate-priced special events regularly and higher-cost endeavors sparingly in our youth group calendars.

"HOW MUCH CAN YOU TYPICALLY AFFORD TO PAY FOR A SPECIAL EVENT WITH YOUR YOUTH GROUP?"

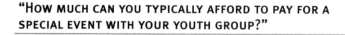

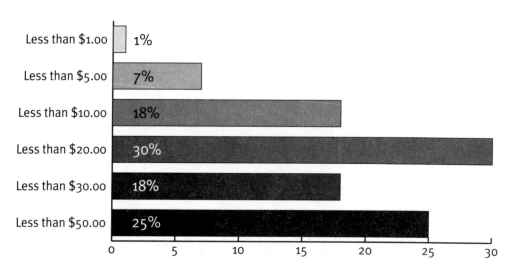

Less than $1.00 — 1%
Less than $5.00 — 7%
Less than $10.00 — 18%
Less than $20.00 — 30%
Less than $30.00 — 18%
Less than $50.00 — 25%

PERCENT OF TEENAGERS WILLING TO PAY UP TO $30 FOR A SPECIAL EVENT, BY REGION AND GENDER

	WILLING TO PAY $10 OR LESS	$20 OR LESS	$30 OR LESS
Eastern/Midwestern	96%	77%	47%
Central/Southern	88%	72%	52%
Southwestern/Western	91%	70%	30%
Males	94%	73%	47%
Females	91%	74%	42%

Entertainment, Evangelism or Both?

As a junior in high school, I became acquainted with an older student named Glenn. Glenn was more interested in experimenting with drugs and alcohol than the things of God. He always smelled like cigarettes and was happy to make disparaging comments about Christians whenever I or others from my church's youth group were around.

In spite of that, Glenn struck up a friendship with another guy from the youth group named Rex. Glenn had heard a tape Rex had of the then-popular Christian music duo, Farrell and Farrell. That was enough to kindle a shared interest.

Glenn couldn't believe that "music this good could be Christian." Soon, he owned the tape himself. A little later in the year, Farrell and Farrell came to our area for a concert. Rex invited Glenn to go to the show with others from our youth ministry. He gladly agreed.

At the concert, Glenn bought a T-shirt, drank in the music and generally had a great time. At the end, Bob Farrell presented the gospel, and for the first time, Glenn actually listened. When Bob invited people to come forward to accept Christ, Glenn hesitated. Then, in one quick motion, he shoved his T-shirt into Rex's lap and went down to pray for salvation with one of the counselors waiting up front.

That experience demonstrates the best of what a youth group special event can accomplish, the providing of a venue in which non-Christian friends of our group members can see the attraction of faith in Christ. God willing, those friends will also join the fold of faith as well.

The question, then, is whether or not our teenagers are finding our events helpful to them in reaching out to their friends. The answer, based on this survey, is encouraging.

> "A LOT OF TEENAGERS—SKATE-BOARDERS—THEY'LL COME IN AND MAYBE THEY'LL COME INTO A CHURCH BUT IT'S KIND OF HARD FOR THEM TO FIT IN. JUST BECAUSE THEY SAY, 'YOU HAVE TO LOOK LIKE THIS. YOU HAVE TO BE LIKE THIS. YOU CAN'T DO THIS.' THERE'S A LOT OF RULES AND REGULATIONS. AND I'M NOT SAYING THAT RULES AND REGULATIONS ARE BAD, BUT TO MAKE AN INFLUENCE ON THEIR LIVES, YOU HAVE TO START LOOKING DOWN AT THE HEART AND SAY, 'WHAT'S THE HEART BEEN THROUGH? WHAT HAVE THEY BEEN THROUGH?' WE NEED TO REACH THEIR HEART INSTEAD OF THEIR CLOTHES."
>
> —EDDIE ELGUERA, FORMER NATIONAL SKATEBOARD CHAMPION AND CURRENT YOUTH PASTOR IN CALIFORNIA[5]

Nearly three-fourths of the students in youth groups just like yours report that the special events you're planning and implementing are either "very helpful" or "somewhat helpful" for reaching their non-Christian friends. That's exciting for two reasons. First, it means we're providing fun, yet spiritually meaningful, events for most of our kids. Second, it means our teens are using those events to spread the kingdom of God into their world.

What about the 27 percent of teenagers (roughly one out of four) who report that our special events are either "little help" or "no help at all" for reaching out to non-Christian students? Theirs is a voice we can't afford to ignore. So I asked these kids to explain why they felt their youth groups' special events provided so little evangelistic help. Here's a sampling of their sad commentary:

"We don't communicate with the non-Christians."

"Sometimes it's hard for my friends to understand [faith in Christ]."

"There are helpful messages, but sometimes those aren't in touch with teens."

"I don't have any non-Christian friends."

"Very few of my friends will come more than once."

"I wouldn't feel comfortable inviting friends to these events."

"These events aren't very interesting."

"My friends hardly buy the Christian faith."

"The gospel is not always presented."

"[Leaders] make the events too childish."

> INTERVIEWER: "WHY DO YOU THINK YOUTH GROUP SPECIAL EVENTS ARE HELPFUL IN REACHING NON-CHRISTIAN FRIENDS?" ANONYMOUS TEENAGER: "BECAUSE I WAS ONCE A NON-CHRISTIAN FRIEND."

"People at church get into arguments with new people."

"Our special events are mostly for fun, not learning about God."

"I don't want to make my friends uncomfortable by pushing God on them, so I don't invite them."

"We don't talk about Christ much at these."

"We don't have many events."

"All our events are without non-Christian friends."

"We're all best friends, so God doesn't come up a lot."

Generally speaking, then, we can feel good about our overall effectiveness in using fun special events to plant seeds of faith in our group members' friends. But judging from the teens' comments above, we also have plenty of room for improvement in this area as well.

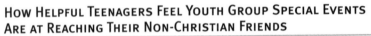

How Helpful Teenagers Feel Youth Group Special Events Are at Reaching Their Non-Christian Friends

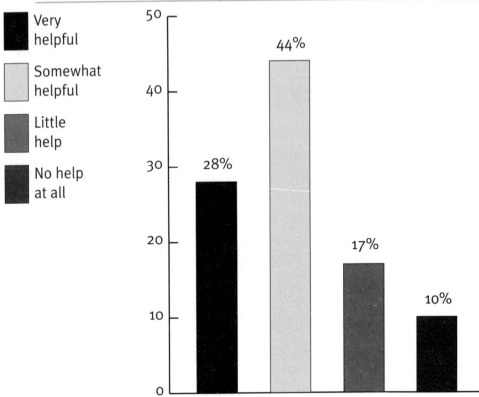

- Very helpful
- Somewhat helpful
- Little help
- No help at all

28% 44% 17% 10%

Chapter Summary and Observations

Lock-ins and Christian music concerts are your best bets for youth group special events.

A couple of youth ministry standards still rank as our students' favorite activities. The great thing about lock-ins is that they are generally low-cost ventures that almost anyone can attend. Since you never get to sleep at these things, put on as many as you can survive!

In addition to large group lock-ins, consider smaller "overnighters" (one for girls only, one for guys only, a seventh-grade-only overnighter and so on) in youth leaders' homes. This will help build community and give a more personal, intimate feel to the activity.

Although generally more expensive, a Christian music concert is one of the easiest events to put on. You collect ticket money from interested students, buy tickets, arrange transportation to and from the concert venue, then let the band do the work.

Check your local Christian bookstore for flyers announcing concerts nearby. A subscription to *CCM Magazine* may also be a worthwhile investment, because in the back of each issue they include a national itinerary of big-name artists such as dc Talk and lesser-known artists such as Soulfood 76.

> "TAKING THE RISK OF BEING CLICHÉD, I WISH EVERY TEENAGER WOULD HAVE THE CHANCE TO HEAR THE GOSPEL AND HAVE THE CHANCE TO MAKE THAT DECISION [FOR CHRIST]."
>
> —DAN HASELTINE, LEAD SINGER FOR JARS OF CLAY[6]

A special event that costs $10 or less is optimum, though many teens will still pay up to $20. Once an event hits $30, it's likely that a majority of your teenagers can't participate.

Simple enough. Budget most of your events to fall in the $20 or less price range and you should be fine. And since everyone likes to splurge once in a while, throw in one or two higher-ticket items as desired.

Three out of four teenagers say a youth group special event is helpful for reaching their non-Christian friends.

FROM A CARTOON BY ROB PORTLOCK: "I THINK WE HAVE EVERYTHING: PAPER PLATES, SODA, COLD CUTS, CHIPS, DIPS, CANDY, NAPKINS, HOT DOGS, HAMBURGERS . . . OOPS! I FORGOT TO INVITE THE YOUTH GROUP!"[7]

For the most part, our teenagers are taking the opportunity afforded by a special event to invite non-Christian friends to join the youth group. Our kids are doing their part to bring their friends; we need to do our part to make faith in Christ a major emphasis at our events as well.

Of course, a formal gospel presentation isn't *always* appropriate, but it *often* is. We can't afford to overlook the opportunity to tell non-Christian teens about Christ.

At your next special event, find a few minutes when the whole group is together—such as just before leaving the church building, midway through a lock-in, on the ride home from a sporting event or just before eating at a pizza night—then take those moments simply to explain the purpose for your group and to offer more information to anyone wanting to know about faith in Jesus. It's that simple and at best is a five-minute proposal—but it's five minutes that can impact eternity.

For Personal Reflection

Take a few moments now to process your own reaction to the information in this chapter. Use these questions to help spark your thinking:

- *Why do you suppose lock-ins rate as the number one special event among Christian teenagers? Did that or any other rating surprise you? Why?*

- *What are ten ways you can make youth group special events more affordable for your teenagers?*

- *What's the best way to present the gospel at a special event? What can you do to incorporate that method in your next youth group event?*

"IT'S FUN, AND YOU CAN BE YOURSELF."

—NINTH GRADER FROM A CHRISTIAN CHURCH, EXPLAINING WHY SHE GOES TO YOUTH GROUP SPECIAL EVENTS

> "SO, BROTHERS AND SISTERS,
>   CHOOSE SEVEN OF YOUR OWN MEN
>   WHO ARE GOOD, FULL OF THE SPIRIT
>   AND FULL OF WISDOM.
> WE WILL PUT THEM IN CHARGE OF THIS WORK."
>   —ACTS 6:3 (NCV)

Chapter 10

WHAT I WISH MY YOUTH LEADER KNEW ABOUT ...

VOLUNTEER LEADERS

Once upon a time there was a man named Mr. Rice who took an interest in young people and volunteered to teach Sunday school for a group of junior highers. He'd been teaching for a while when a boy joined the class.

Twelve-year-old Norman Wakefield was unfamiliar with church, but through the influence of a woman who worked in a candy store, Norman began attending Sunday school. Painfully shy and a little smaller than the other students, this young man was at first uncomfortable in Sunday school. Still, there was something about him the volunteer leader couldn't let go. He took an interest in Norm and taught him the Bible as best he could.

> "THE VOLUNTEER LEADERS IN MY YOUTH GROUP HAVE MADE A VERY HUMONGOUS IMPACT ON MY RELATIONSHIP WITH GOD. . . . THERE'S ONE LEADER—SHE'S LIKE A MOTHER TO ME. I CAN TALK TO HER ABOUT ANYTHING. [THE LEADERS] ARE PROBABLY MY BEST FRIENDS."
>
> —TWELFTH-GRADE FEMALE FROM A NON-DENOMINATIONAL CHURCH IN MICHIGAN

Finally, Mr. Rice got up the nerve to explain to this awkward 12-year-old how Jesus died on the cross to pay for our sins and how Jesus rose from the dead to give us eternal life. The teacher asked Norm if he'd like to accept that gift of forgiveness and eternal life Jesus offers. To his (and Heaven's) delight, Norm accepted, and the teacher led the boy in accepting Jesus.

About a year later, due to family difficulties, Norman was sent 125 miles away to live with his grandparents for a while. While Norm was away, Mr. Rice moved to Tennessee, and the teacher and student lost contact with each other. They were never reunited.

But Norm never forgot the moment when a volunteer youth leader led him to Christ. He studied the Scriptures through his teen years and was instrumental in leading his own family members to faith in Jesus.

> "YOU HAVE TO START IN THE CHURCH, I THINK. THAT'S WHERE YOU CAN FIND THE BEST LEADERS."
>
> —SUPER BOWL CHAMPION FULL-BACK, HOWARD GRIFFITH, OF THE DENVER BRONCOS, TALKING ABOUT WHERE TEENAGERS SHOULD LOOK FOR ROLE MODELS[1]

Upon graduating from high school, he went to Bible college. He even became a youth pastor for a while! A fire burned inside him, and wherever he went, Norm spread that flame of faith to others, touching people here, touching people there and encouraging them to go and touch even more people.

Norm went on to seminary and continued his church involvement. Eventually he became a seminary professor and a pastor, training future pastors, youth pastors, missionaries and more. Over the years his students included Christian leaders such as Neil T. Anderson and Pastor Darrell DelHousaye, as well as thousands of other "unknown" Christian leaders still at work today.

All told, young Norman's influence has now spanned several generations and impacted literally millions of people for Christ's kingdom—and continues to impact more each day.[2]

I tell you this true story to make one point: *Volunteer leaders matter.*

Imagine how many lives—maybe even yours!—might be poorer if more than fifty years ago there was no volunteer Sunday school teacher who cared enough to lead junior-high boys to Christ. Now imagine how much poorer your ministry would be without those kinds of volunteers today.

Since volunteer leaders have the power to effect this broad a reach of influence, I felt it was important to finish out the survey by asking teenagers their thoughts about their leaders. I wanted to know: 1) *really*, how much influence these leaders bear on students' church involvement, 2) what kinds of qualities teenagers wanted you, their youth leaders, to look for in volunteer leaders and 3) what teens really feel about having their parents involved in youth group leadership.

Thankfully, these teenagers were happy to share their opinions.

> "WE TEND TO FOCUS ON THE *OBJECTS* OF MINISTRY: THE SOULS LED TO CHRIST, THE MARRIAGES RESCUED, THE POOR FED AND HOUSED, THE HOMEBOUND ELDERLY VISITED, THE TEENAGERS CHALLENGED. YET AS I READ THE NEW TESTAMENT, JESUS SEEMS EQUALLY INTERESTED IN WHAT EFFECT MINISTRY IS HAVING ON THE PEOPLE WHO ARE DOING THE WORK OF MINISTRY THEMSELVES."
>
> —PHILIP YANCEY[3]

The Verdict Is In!

My good friend Mikal Keefer is a volunteer youth worker by night and a marketing guru by day. I asked him once to tell me about direct-mail campaigns—you know, the so-called "junk mail" that regularly floods your mailbox.

Mikal informed me that most of those campaigns send out a mass mailing advertisement and/or letter and hope that will influence a surprisingly small percentage of recipients to respond.

"Generally speaking, a 2 percent response is respectable," Mikal said. "And a 5 percent response is very good."

In other words, if the marketing method they are using to reach their audience yields only a 5 percent effectiveness rate, that still is a healthy, productive method.

Compare that to youth ministry. Our number one method for reaching teenagers isn't postcards or even flashy events—it's people! Typically those people within our church who are willing to volunteer their time and resources to our ministry.

Now, judging by marketing standards, if only 5 percent of our teenagers were influenced to become involved in our youth group because of a volunteer leader, that'd be a good return. In actuality, however, we're seeing a much greater return—a return that would make any marketer green with envy!

FROM A CARTOON BY RANDY GLASBERGEN: "OUR CHURCH YOUTH GROUP LEADER IS A GREAT GUY WITH A LOT OF ENERGY, WHO REALLY RELATES WELL TO KIDS. EITHER THAT, OR HE'S JUST IMMATURE!"[4]

When I asked teenagers about volunteer leaders, three out of every four students (76%) told me their leaders exerted a "moderate" or "great deal" of influence on their youth group participation. Another 14 percent admitted that although their youth volunteers weren't a major influence, they did exert "a little." That means, for 90 percent of the students we serve, a volunteer leader is making a difference.

That's exciting! It reaffirms for us that God is still using *people* to meet the needs of people. It also makes it clear that the days of the "one-man show" type of ministry are a thing of the past. To maximize the potential of our youth ministry, we need to maximize our volunteer base.

When I worked in full-time youth ministry, I noticed an interesting trend at each of my churches. The number of students in my youth group always grew in direct proportion to the number of volunteer leaders I had on staff. At most any time of the year, I could take the number of volunteers I had involved in the lives of kids, multiply that by a number between six and ten, and that was roughly the number of youth regularly involved in my youth group. (Try that little formula for yourself now. Does it work for your group too?)

If the students who took this survey were being honest, that correlation between group members and youth leaders was no coincidence. Volunteer leaders matter to our teenagers, which means if we want to grow a youth group numerically, we need to grow our volunteer staff first.

Among the teenagers surveyed, the influence of volunteers fluctuated somewhat by grade, with generally 33 to 42 percent of each grade reporting their leaders exerted "a great deal" of influence. The notable exception, though, is among our twelfth graders. For seniors, more than half (51%) report that their leaders influence them a great deal when it comes to youth group involvement.

> "WHEN OUR VOLUNTEER LEADERS GIVE THEIR TESTIMONIES, I REALLY RESPECT THAT AND LOOK UP TO THEM. THEY'RE THERE FOR US."
>
> —TENTH GRADER FROM A METHODIST CHURCH

Possible explanations vary. Perhaps, as seniors, they've had more time to get to know the long-term volunteers. Perhaps, with graduation just around the corner, they're more interested in finding and keeping mentors to help them transition to adulthood. Perhaps, because twelfth graders act more like adults, youth leaders are unconsciously investing more time in seniors. Whatever the reason, we need to be careful to provide the leaders those students want and need.

"AS A WHOLE, HOW MUCH INFLUENCE DO VOLUNTEER LEADERS HAVE ON YOUR LEVEL OF INVOLVEMENT IN YOUR YOUTH GROUP?"

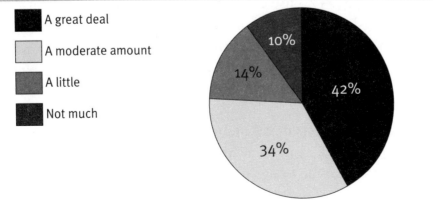

- A great deal
- A moderate amount
- A little
- Not much

10%
14%
42%
34%

**PERCENT OF TEENAGERS WHO SAY VOLUNTEER LEADERS INFLUENCE THEIR
LEVEL OF INVOLVEMENT IN YOUTH GROUP "A GREAT DEAL," BY GRADE**

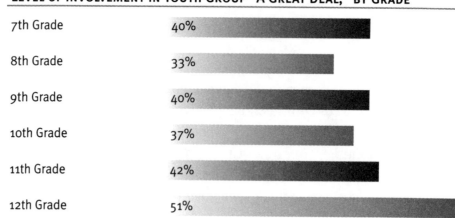

7th Grade	40%
8th Grade	33%
9th Grade	40%
10th Grade	37%
11th Grade	42%
12th Grade	51%

May I Take Your Order, Please?

So what kind of volunteer leaders do our students really want? The survey listed twelve character traits, and students were asked to choose the two traits that best describe the kind of person they want their youth pastors to select. Here's what they said:

The number one character quality teenagers desire in their volunteer staffers is a "commitment to Jesus"—plain and simple. Just under half of all teenagers (44%) listed this choice. That tells me that our teens don't want a leader who can simply teach them about faith, they want someone who can *model* that faith. Our students want to see what faith in Jesus looks, sounds and feels like. And they want to experience that through our example and the example of our staff.

This data also suggests a real desire among teenagers for Christian mentors, people who can come alongside and shepherd them, who can encourage them in the things of God and help them grow. Our students want leaders who are traveling the same faith journey as themselves—but a few steps ahead. What an honor—and what a responsibility.

The second-ranking quality our young people listed was a "caring attitude." About one in three teens (32%) chose this option. When I look at this choice in conjunction with their number one choice, it strikes me that these two qualities clearly reflect Jesus' words in Matthew 22:37-39:

"'Love the Lord your God with all your heart and with all your soul and with all your mind.' This is the first and greatest commandment. And the second is like it: 'Love your neighbor as yourself.'"

> "ONE OF THE VOLUNTEERS—I'M TRYING TO START PLAYING THE GUITAR—HE'S HELPING WITH THAT SO I CAN PLAY IN OUR PRAISE AND WORSHIP GROUP. BESIDES, HE'S OLDER AND MATURE, AND IT HELPS TO HAVE HIS INPUT ON CERTAIN THINGS."
> —NINTH-GRADE MALE FROM INDIANA

Love the Lord—be committed to Jesus. Love your neighbor—care about others. Both of the qualities teenagers listed highest resonate with the spirit of Jesus' commands. I'm awed to find out that what our teenagers want most in their leaders is simply people who are living what should be a normal Christian's life by following Jesus' greatest commands.

Now, lest we get too spiritual, let's take a look at the third character quality teenagers most desire in their leaders: FUN! That's right, in youth ministry you can have fun and still be a Christian! With about one in four kids (24%) choosing "fun-loving" from the survey, they're serving notice that they want to enjoy life and they want to do it at church.

Funny thing, God wants us to enjoy life too. In fact, the word "joy" is listed 210 times in the NIV translation of Scripture. So the lesson for us, then, is to seek out as volunteers those individuals who have a healthy sense of fun, who can enjoy being alive and being with teenagers. (OK, go ahead and put a sign on the youth group door now that says "No Grouches Allowed!")

The one other quality that pulled significant, though not overwhelming, support was "encouraging personality." One in five teenagers (21%) rated this among their top two choices. To put it in the vernacular of Winnie the Pooh's Hundred Acre Wood, they'd rather be discipled by Christopher Robin than Eeyore. So when you're looking for volunteers, keep a sharp eye out for adults who are more apt to build a teenager up, not unintentionally knock a youth down.

No discussion of what teenagers care about in a youth leader is complete without at least a glance at what students *don't* care about.

Generally speaking, a leader's age is a nonfactor among teenagers. Only 7 percent said a volunteer should be "not too old," and less than 1 percent said a volunteer shouldn't be "too young." Likewise teenagers are unconcerned about a leader's "loyalty" and "wisdom"—although my gut feeling with the loyalty response is that leaders are rarely disloyal, so students aren't worrying about it.

Perhaps the most telling, though not really surprising, quality teenagers viewed with little regard was a leader's ability to teach. Only one out of twenty teens (5%) rated this as important, showing us again our teenagers aren't so interested in *what* a youth leader can do but *who* that youth leader is as a person and mentor. And hopefully he or she is a committed Christian with a caring and fun-loving attitude.

"WHAT QUALITIES DO YOU WANT YOUR YOUTH PASTOR TO LOOK FOR MOST WHEN HE OR SHE IS SELECTING A VOLUNTEER YOUTH LEADER?" (CIRCLE UP TO TWO ITEMS.)

Quality	Percent
Commitment to Jesus	44%
Caring attitude	32%
Fun-loving	24%
Encouraging personality	21%
Good listener	11%
Well-informed of teen trends	11%
Honesty	10%
Not too old	7%
Good teacher	5%
Wisdom	5%
Loyalty	4%
Not too young	<1%

The Parent Trap

I have a confession to make at this juncture of the chapter. For many years I've been a strong advocate of using teenagers' own parents as volunteer youth leaders. My thinking was: a) Parents are typically hands-on experts on teenagers and teen culture—they have a "sample" in their own homes; b) It's good for parents to be involved in the lives of their kids, and youth group is a great place to be involved; c) Youth may grumble at first but will get used to seeing mom or dad around and may even come to enjoy it; and d) It's healthy for other teenagers to see a parent and his or her teenage child relating to each other in a setting where the teen is in charge of the environment. But, when confronted with the results of this survey, I have to admit that a significant portion of teenagers don't seem to agree with my opinion!

Now, I'm not suggesting that we kick every parent out of our youth rooms or that we dismiss immediately any parent wishing to serve. But

I am saying that the results of this portion of the survey indicate that we need to be careful and involve teenagers themselves when making a decision about whether or not to have a parent actively involved as a youth leader.

Here's why I've had to change my perspective on this issue. When teens were asked how many supported the idea of their parents volunteering in the youth group, just under one in five (19%) said they did. By contrast, when asked how many were against the idea, nearly half of all teenagers (46%) said they opposed having their parents hanging around the youth room.

"Oh, you know, that's probably just kids with strong feelings in one region who wrecked the curve," I thought. Then I checked the data from each region. Although not exactly the same, they were remarkably consistent, with around 45 percent opposing and roughly 20 percent in each region supporting parents as youth leaders. Next I checked by gender and found that regardless of whether they're male or female, teenagers still oppose having their parents lead in youth group by a two-to-one margin—or more.

> "I'VE NEVER HEARD A LEADER SAY, 'DON'T ENCOURAGE ME ANYMORE. I'VE HAD ALL I CAN HANDLE. I CAN'T TAKE ANY MORE APPRECIATION.'"
>
> —DOUG FIELDS[5]

So I pulled out my last line of defense. "Well," I thought, "I'll bet the kids who said their volunteer leaders exert a great influence on their youth group involvement *really* want parents there. In fact, I'm sure of it!"

So I ran the data again, comparing teens' responses to the influence question with their answers to the question about parents. The result? Among teenagers who say they are influenced "a great deal" by their volunteer leaders, about half (49%) oppose having a parent as one of those volunteers! So much for this theory.

At that point I figured it was time to admit defeat—and perhaps you need to admit that too. Regardless of what we want to believe, the data indicates that teenagers have a strong sentiment against parental involvement in their youth groups.

Of course, there are exceptions—those brave one in five students who actually want parents in their youth group. But for the most part, we'd be wise to listen to our students and use parents sparingly, if possible. (Just tell them their greatest contribution to your youth ministry happens at their homes anyway!)

"WHICH STATEMENT BEST DESCRIBES HOW YOU'D FEEL ABOUT YOUR PARENTS BEING VOLUNTEER LEADERS IN YOUR YOUTH GROUP?"

"I'm strongly for the idea"	7%
"I'm moderately for the idea"	12%
"Makes no difference to me"	35%
"I'm moderately against the idea"	23%
"I'm strongly against the idea"	23%

AMONG TEENAGERS WHO SAY VOLUNTEER LEADERS EXERT "A GREAT DEAL" OF INFLUENCE ON THEIR LEVEL OF YOUTH GROUP INVOLVEMENT . . .

49% are "strongly against" or "moderately against" parents serving as volunteer leaders.

21% are "strongly for" or "moderately for" parents serving as volunteer leaders.

AMONG TEENAGERS WHO SAY VOLUNTEER LEADERS EXERT "NOT MUCH" INFLUENCE ON THEIR LEVEL OF YOUTH GROUP INVOLVEMENT . . .

40% are "strongly against" or "moderately against" parents serving as volunteer leaders.

22% are "strongly for" or "moderately for" parents serving as volunteer leaders.

Chapter Summary and Observations

Volunteer leaders exert a tremendous influence on how involved your teenagers are in your youth group.

This is both good news and bad news. The good news is that you've got at your fingertips an excellent tool for reaching teenagers—people. The bad news is that sometimes that "people resource" is hard to come by.

> "I DIDN'T REALLY BELIEVE IN GOD, AND WHEN I CAME HERE THE LEADERS HELPED ME FEEL LIKE A PART OF THE GROUP AND IN THE PAST YEAR I'VE REALLY BUILT A STRONG RELATIONSHIP WITH GOD."
>
> —TENTH GRADER FROM MISSOURI

Still, this reaffirms one youth ministry principle we need to take to heart: If we want to invest deeply into the lives of teenagers, we need to invest heavily in our volunteer leaders, then trust them and God to multiply that investment in our students.

Teenagers want youth leaders who are committed, caring and fun.

In short, they're looking for mentors who can model a normal Christian life characterized by faithfulness, love and joy. Unfortunately, a "normal" Christian is sometimes hard to come by, so where do you find these people?

I'm convinced prayer is the answer to that question. If we believe God truly wants our young people to benefit from positive role models in our ministry, we must trust God to bring those people in. Of course, I'm not suggesting we suspend all recruiting efforts and become lackadaisical in our constant search for volunteers. But I am proposing we go to God first with our staffing needs and ask him to plant our youth ministries on the hearts of potential leaders in such a way that they'll respond to his call.

I don't tell you this just out of "theory." I've seen it happen in practice. The church I currently attend went through a famine of youth leaders for about two years. The youth pastor was overworked, we volunteer staffers had our hands full and there were still many unmet needs in our group. We tried all the typical strategies—announcements, phone calls, stories of mournful teenagers, etc. Still, very few people came forward.

Finally, in one of our staff meetings, a leader said, "I believe God wants these teenagers to have leaders. But I also believe it's not our job to manipulate people into serving. If we want more leaders, we need to go to the source that brought each of us into this group in the first place. We need to go to God."

From that point on, we quit all our nifty, crafty, manipulative tactics for recruiting volunteers and even required a higher commitment from new leaders. And all the time we used to spend strategizing, we now spent praying. Within eight months, all our staffing needs were filled, and the people who filled them all had the same story: "I wasn't even thinking about working with teenagers, but for some reason I can't seem to get these kids off my heart lately. Is there anything I can do to help out in the youth group?"

Do you want leaders who are committed, caring and fun? Get on your knees and ask the divine Recruiter to bring those people into your youth ministry.

Generally speaking, your teenagers will be more comfortable without their parents in the youth group.

Perhaps they feel more free to discuss their problems (which can often include struggles with parents anyway), or perhaps they just want to be in an environment where they're independent. Regardless, teenagers apparently feel strongly about not having their parents as their youth leaders. Whenever possible, accommodate that sentiment.

But what do you do if you have a parent who would otherwise be a great youth leader, but that has a teenager in your group? I'd suggest three things:

1) Talk to the teenager to find out how he or she feels. Maybe that student is one of the minority who really prefers a parent in youth ministry leadership. If that's the case, you're home free—put that mom or dad to work! However, if you sense some hesitancy, either spoken or unspoken, be sensitive to that and choose the teenager's preference over the parent's.

2) Look for ways to involve parents that don't require much direct involvement with teenagers. For example, use parents as consultants for annual planning and strategy; as travel and meal coordinators; as drivers who take younger students to and from events; as editors of the youth group newsletter; as phone callers who get updates out quickly; as bulletin-board caretakers; as artists for flyers, invitations and posters; as child-care workers for other volunteer leaders; as fund-raisers; as construction workers (don't you need a sand-volleyball pit somewhere on church grounds?); as secret pals for your students; and, of course, as pray-ers for the teens in your care.

The point is, just because a teenager may not want his or her parent at youth meetings, doesn't mean a parent can't find some other way to serve—and make a difference—in youth ministry at your church.

3) Take a rain check. There is no youth ministry rule that mandates expiration dates for offers to serve. Express heartfelt appreciation for a parent's desire to help out, then ask that he or she wait until after that mom or dad's child has left the youth group. (Or until the teenager is

comfortable having the parent there.) Barring any unforeseen disaster, your youth group and that parent will still be there long after that teenager is gone.

The benefits of waiting are worth the cost. After all, *every* teenager—present and future—needs a volunteer willing to make an impact in his or her life. Who knows? A parent who waits to minister today may, five years from now, be the person who influences a group member who will in turn impact millions someday.

For Personal Reflection

Take a few moments now to process your own reaction to the information in this chapter. Use these questions to help spark your thinking:

- *What three qualities best characterize your current youth staff as a whole? How does that compare to what teenagers say they want in volunteer leaders?*

- *Why do you suppose teenagers are so strongly opposed to having their parents as youth leaders? How does that impact your volunteer staffing plans?*

- *Looking back through this book as a whole, what information did you find the most helpful? How will reading this book make an impact on your youth ministry?*

AFTERWORD: NOW WHAT?

As I finish the writing of *What I Wish My Youth Leader Knew About Youth Ministry,* I realize there are still a few things I want to share with you about me personally. For instance, I've written this entire book in bed.

No, it's not just that I'm extremely lazy. In December of 1996, I first began to feel the effects of a rare, chronic stomach disorder that wasn't diagnosed until many months later. Because of this disorder, I battle nausea on a daily basis. As you can guess, that seriously limits what I can and can't do. In fact, it delayed the writing (and therefore the release) of this very book.

Now, I don't want you to think that I'm an invalid wasting away in my bedroom, because I'm not. Thanks to a handful of medicines and a concerned doctor, I'm often able to function almost normally. In fact, if you met me, you might not notice anything was wrong except that I'm very particular about when I eat. (I can eat only when my medicine is in full force.)

But the biggest change this illness has caused is that for the first time in many years, I'm no longer able to work on the front lines of youth ministry. I tried for a while, but my health made my attendance so erratic that I finally had to walk away.

That has been very difficult for me. I love teenagers in general, and the kids at my church are especially important to me. When I was in the hospital, it was these kids who prayed for me. When I came home and tried to adjust to a change in lifestyle, it was these kids who visited me, encouraged me, cheered me and still continued to pray for me. Now, months after my last youth group meeting, these kids still stop me in the hall at church to ask how I'm doing, to remind me that they're praying for a miracle and just to chat.

Last Sunday, I came home from church very discouraged that I can't be very involved in their lives anymore, at least for now. Then I remembered something.

You still can.

When I'm sitting at home on Sunday nights, you might be leading a small group at your church. On Wednesdays, you could be leading a rowdy game with teenagers or joining kids in worship. This weekend, you might be taking your kids on a ski trip, or to the beach or just out for a Coke.

And I thought, I can't work the front lines, but I *can* give something to those who do. And so I give you this book. Please use it, refer back to it, tear the binding a little from overuse, highlight things that mean something to your ministry, jot "he's nuts!" notes in the margin where you disagree and think I've gone off the deep end.

When you see an idea from this book that actually bears a little fruit in your ministry, remember to share it with someone else. Because you never know, there may come a day when you're sidelined from a ministry with teenagers. If that happens, you, like me, will be encouraged to know that somewhere out there, somebody is making a difference in the lives of teenagers—and maybe something you said is helping them do that.

Mike Nappa
Spring 1998

ENDNOTES

Introduction

[1]George Barna, *The Second Coming of the Church* (Nashville: Word Publishing, 1998), p. 71.
[2]William Strauss and Neil Howe, *Generations* (New York: William Morrow and Company, 1991), p. 36.
[3]Mike Nappa, Amy Nappa and Michael Warden, *Get Real: Making Core Christian Beliefs Relevant to Teenagers* (Loveland, CO: Group Publishing, 1996), pp. 8-12.
[4]William Strauss and Neil Howe, *The Fourth Turning* (New York: Broadway Books, 1997), p. 234.
[5]Neil Howe and Bill Strauss, *13th Gen: Abort, Retry, Ignore, Fail?* (New York: Vintage Books, 1993), p. 17.
[6]*The World Almanac and Book of Facts 1997* (Mahwah, NJ: World Almanac Books, 1996), p. 379.
[7]Strauss and Howe, *Generations*, p. 336.
[8]Ibid.
[9]Strauss and Howe, *The Fourth Turning*, p. 245.
[10]Ibid.
[11]Strauss and Howe, *Generations*, pp. 335-343.

Chapter 1

[1]George Barna, *The Second Coming of the Church* (Nashville: Word Publishing, 1998), pp. 3, 4.
[2]Anthony Campolo, foreword to *How to Speak to Youth*, by Ken Davis (Loveland, CO: Group Publishing, 1986), p. 6.
[3]Jars of Clay, interviewed by the author, Estes Park, CO, July 30, 1997.
[4]Barna, *The Second Coming of the Church*, p. 186.
[5]Todd Peterson, telephone conversation with the author, September 17, 1997.
[6]Thom and Joani Schultz, *Why Nobody Learns Much of Anything at Church: and How to Fix It* (Loveland, CO: Group Publishing, 1993), p. 143.
[7]Davis, *How to Speak to Youth*, p. 94.

Chapter 2

[1]Philip Yancey, *Church: Why Bother?* (Grand Rapids, MI: Zondervan Publishing House, 1998), p. 25.
[2]Mike and Amy Nappa, *52 Fun Family Prayer Adventures* (Minneapolis: Augsburg Books, 1996), p. 70.
[3]Ibid.
[4]Keith Anderson, e-mail interview with the author, September 1997.
[5]Robin Jones Gunn, e-mail interview with the author, October 1997.
[6]Doug Hall, *Less Than Entirely Sanctified* (Downers Grove, IL: InterVarsity Press, 1992), p. 26.
[7]*Some Kind of Journey: On the Road With Audio Adrenaline*, ed. Dale Reeves (Cincinnati, OH: Standard Publishing, 1997), p. 38.
[8]Steven Curtis Chapman, telephone conversation with the author, June 18, 1996.
[9]Rebecca St. James, *40 Days With God: A Devotional Journey* (Cincinnati, OH: Standard Publishing, 1996), p. 71.
[10]*Some Kind of Journey: On the Road With Audio Adrenaline*, ed. Dale Reeves, pp. 43, 45.

Chapter 3

[1]Quoted in *All-Star Games From All-Star Youth Leaders* (Loveland, CO: Group Publishing, 1998), p. 27.
[2]Wayne Rice and Mike Yaconelli, *Play It!* (Grand Rapids, MI: Zondervan Publishing House, 1986), p. 17.
[3]Quoted in *All-Star Games From All-Star Youth Leaders*, p. 14.
[4]Eugene C. Roehlkepartain, *Youth Ministry in City Churches* (Loveland, CO: Group Publishing, 1989), p. 148.

[5]Quoted in *The Complete Book of Everyday Christianity*, ed. Robert Banks and R. Paul Stevens (Downers Grove, IL: InterVarsity Press, 1997), p. 443.
[6]Quoted in *All-Star Games From All-Star Youth Leaders*, p. 55.
[7]Quoted in *All-Star Games From All-Star Youth Leaders*, p. 63.

Chapter 4

[1]Bob Briner and Ray Pritchard, *The Leadership Lessons of Jesus* (Nashville: Broadman & Holman, 1997), p. 43.
[2]*Fresh Illustrations for Preaching and Teaching From Leadership Journal*, ed. Edward K. Rowell (Grand Rapids, MI: Baker Books, 1997), p. 201.
[3]*PastorPoll™ 1997* (Oxnard, CA: Barna Research Group, Ltd., August 1997), p. 4.
[4]"Barna Survey Reveals Current Statistics on Protestant Churches," Zondervan Publishing House E-mail Alert Service (November 5, 1997), p. 2.
[5]*Clip-Art Cartoons for Churches*, ed. Mike Nappa (Loveland, CO: Group Publishing, 1995), p. 81.
[6]Peter Benson and Carolyn Elkin, *Effective Christian Education, Summary Report* (Minneapolis: Search Institute, 1990), p. 2.
[7]*God's Little Devotional Book on Prayer* (Tulsa, OK: Honor Books, 1997), p. 36.
[8]Thom and Joani Schultz, *Why Nobody Learns Much of Anything at Church: And How to Fix It* (Loveland, CO: Group Publishing, 1993), p. 109.
[9]Mike Nappa, Amy Nappa and Michael Warden, *Get Real: Making Core Christian Beliefs Relevant to Teenagers* (Loveland, CO: Group Publishing, 1996), p. 139.
[10]E. M. Bounds, *Purpose in Prayer* (Chicago: Moody Press, 1909), p. 7.
[11]Schultz, *Why Nobody Learns Much of Anything at Church*, p. 227.
[12]George Barna, *The Second Coming of the Church* (Nashville: Word Publishing, 1998), p. 10.
[13]Philip Yancey, *Church: Why Bother?* (Grand Rapids, MI: Zondervan Publishing House, 1998), p. 21.
[14]Doug Hall, *Less Than Entirely Sanctified* (Downers Grove, IL: InterVarsity Press, 1992), p. 4.
[15]Quoted in *Fresh Illustrations for Preaching and Teaching From Leadership Journal*, p. 201.

Chapter 5

[1]Larnelle Harris, e-mail interview with Amy Nappa, January 22, 1998.
[2]Anne Fisher, "If You Really *Don't* Want the Job . . .", *Reader's Digest,* volume 151, number 908 (December 1997), p. 94.
[3]George Barna, *The Second Coming of the Church* (Nashville: Word Publishing, 1998), p. 18.
[4]Quoted in Michael Warden, "Generational Trends," *Vital Ministry 1* (January–February 1998), p. 69.
[5]Carman, telephone conversation with the author, November 2, 1995.
[6]Quoted in *God's Little Devotion Book on Prayer* (Tulsa, OK: Honor Books, 1997), p. 56.

Chapter 6

[1]Doug Fields, *Purpose-Driven Youth Ministry* (Grand Rapids, MI: Zondervan Publishing House, 1998), p. 140.
[2]Bruce Fretts, "Robert Duvall," *Entertainment Weekly* (February 13, 1998), pp. 24-26.
[3]Fields, *Purpose-Driven Youth Ministry,* pp. 140-142.
[4]Bo Boshers, with Kim Anderson, *Student Ministry for the 21st Century* (Grand Rapids, MI: Zondervan Publishing House, 1997), p. 174.
[5]Ron Nicholas et al., *Small Group Leaders' Handbook* (Downers Grove, IL: InterVarsity Press, 1982), p. 37.
[6]George Barna, *Virtual America* (Ventura, CA: Regal Books, 1994), p. 53.
[7]George Barna, *Generation Next* (Ventura, CA: Regal Books, 1995), p. 88.
[8]Nicholas et al., *Small Group Leaders' Handbook,* p. 48.
[9]Quoted in "'Dead Man Walking' Author Visits Oklahoma City," *Loveland Reporter-Herald*, February 18, 1998.

[10]*God's Little Devotional Book II* (Tulsa, OK: Honor Books, 1997), p. 209.
[11]Susie Shellenberger, telephone conversation with the author, April 2, 1996.
[12]Quoted in Nancy Rubin, *Ask Me If I Care* (Berkeley, CA: Ten Speed Press, 1994), p. 158.
[13]George Barna, *The Second Coming of the Church* (Nashville: Word Publishing, 1998), p. 187.

Chapter 7

[1]John McPherson, *McPherson Goes to Church* (Grand Rapids, MI: Zondervan Publishing House, 1994), p. 108.
[2]Jars of Clay, interviewed by the author, Estes Park, CO, July 30, 1997.
[3]Paul Borthwick, *Organizing Your Youth Ministry* (Grand Rapids, MI: Zondervan Publishing House, 1988), p. 148.
[4]Ibid.
[5]E. G. von Trutzschler, *Outrageous Object Lessons* (Ventura, CA: Gospel Light, 1987), pp. 38, 39.
[6]Al McKay and R. Paul Stevens, "Camping," in *The Complete Book of Everyday Christianity*, ed. Robert Banks and R. Paul Stevens (Downers Grove, IL: InterVarsity Press, 1997), p. 103.
[7]Todd Peterson, telephone conversation with the author, September 17, 1997.
[8]John Pearson, "Weekend Retreats," in *The Youth Leader's Source Book*, ed. Gary Dausey (Grand Rapids, MI: Zondervan Publishing House, 1983), p. 210.
[9]Quoted in *The Book of Wisdom* (Sisters, OR: Multnomah Publishers, 1997), p. 449.

Chapter 8

[1]Peter L. Benson and Eugene C. Roehlkepartain, *Beyond Leaf Raking* (Nashville: Abingdon Press, 1993), p. 15.
[2]Jim Burns and Greg McKinnon, *Illustrations, Stories, and Quotes to Hang Your Message On* (Ventura, CA: Gospel Light, 1997), p. 159.
[3]Benson and Roehlkepartain, *Beyond Leaf Raking*, pp. 15-29.
[4]Ibid., p. 22.
[5]Rich Mullins, telephone conversation with the author, February 15, 1996.
[6]Benson and Roehlkepartain, *Beyond Leaf Raking*, p. 30.
[7]Ronald J. Sider, *Rich Christians in an Age of Hunger* (Nashville: Word Publishing, 1997), p. xiv.

Chapter 9

[1]Audio Adrenaline, interviewed by the author, Denver, CO, May 7, 1996.
[2]Rebecca St. James, *40 Days With God: A Devotional Journey* (Cincinnati, OH: Standard Publishing, 1996), p. 39.
[3]Amy Nappa, "What's News," *Group's Retreat, Trip, and Travel Guide*, 1998 edition, p. 5.
[4]*Clip-Art Cartoons for Churches*, ed. Mike Nappa (Loveland, CO: Group Publishing, 1995), p. 63.
[5]Eddie Elguera, telephone conversation with the author, December 1, 1997.
[6]Jars of Clay, interviewed by the author, Estes Park, CO, July 30, 1997.
[7]*Clip-Art Cartoons for Churches*, p. 101.

Chapter 10

[1]Howard Griffith, interviewed by the author, Greeley, CO, August 11, 1997.
[2]Norman Wakefield, telephone conversation with the author, January 1998.
[3]Philip Yancey, *Church: Why Bother?* (Grand Rapids, MI: Zondervan Publishing House, 1998), p. 80.
[4]*Clip-Art Cartoons for Churches*, ed. Mike Nappa (Loveland, CO: Group Publishing, 1995), p. 111.
[5]Doug Fields, *Purpose-Driven Youth Ministry* (Grand Rapids, MI: Zondervan Publishing House, 1998), p. 302.

APPENDIX 1: THE SURVEY

Congratulations! You've been chosen to participate in a national survey to educate youth leaders on what teenagers really want and need in a youth group. Your answers will be used to create a book titled, *What I Wish My Youth Leader Knew About Youth Ministry*, which will release next year. Please answer each question that follows carefully, honestly and neatly so your youth leaders can learn how to do their jobs better. Thanks!

•••

DEMOGRAPHICS:

What grade in school are you in?
What state do you live in? (i.e., Arizona, New York, etc.)
What is your church affiliation? (i.e., Baptist, Catholic, etc.)
Are you male or female?

•••

TOPICAL QUESTIONS:

1. How long do you think is best for a typical youth talk or sermon?
a) less than 15 minutes   b) between 15-30 minutes
c) between 30-45 minutes   d) between 45-60 minutes
e) more than an hour

2. Finish this sentence: I learn most from a youth talk/sermon when it includes . . . (circle up to two items)
a) discussion   b) learning activities
c) stories   d) lecture only
e) skits/drama   f) formal Scripture readings
g) other (please list here)

3. Finish this sentence: I prefer youth talks that . . . (circle one)
a) focus on real-life topics first and then apply appropriate Scriptures
b) focus on a certain passage of Scripture first and then apply it to
   real-life situations

4. Finish this sentence: On the whole, the time our youth group
   regularly spends in worship is . . . (circle one)
a) not enough   b) about right   c) too much

5. Which forms of worship does your group most often participate in?
   (circle up to two)
a) group singing   b) silence
c) prayers of thanks and praise   d) Scripture readings
e) service projects   f) liturgical dance
g) other (please list here)

6. Which forms of worship do you like most? (circle up to two)
a) group singing   b) silence
c) prayers of thanks and praise   d) Scripture readings
e) service projects   f) liturgical dance
g) other (please list here)

7. Which do you like best during a time of group singing?
a) singing mostly hymns
b) singing mostly praise songs
c) singing mostly contemporary Christian songs
d) other (please list here)

8. How important to you are crowdbreakers and games in a youth group?
a) very important
b) moderately important
c) slightly important
d) not important at all

9. Which words best describe the crowdbreakers and games your youth group generally uses? (circle up to two)

a) fun   b) complicated   c) creative

d) childish   e) affirming   f) boring

g) competitive   h) cooperative   i) embarrassing

j) relationship-building   k) other (please list here)

10. Which game styles do you like best? (circle up to two)

a) relays   b) team competitions

c) individual competitions   d) physical/active games

e) mental games   f) noncompetitive games

g) sports-related games   h) elimination games

i) word games   j) other (please list here)

11. Finish this sentence: Sunday school is . . .

a) not much help in my spiritual growth

b) sometimes helpful in my spiritual growth

c) occasionally helpful in my spiritual growth

d) often helpful in my spiritual growth

12. Which words best describe your Sunday school experience? (circle up to two)

a) exciting   b) boring   c) deep   d) out-of-touch

e) simple   f) challenging g) time-waster h) valuable

i) passive   j) interactive k) trite   l) thought-provoking

m) other (please list here)

13. What does your group spend the most time on during Sunday school?

a) discussion   b) hearing a speaker   c) learning activities

d) worksheets   e) prayer   f) Bible reading

g) other (please list here)

14. How comfortable do you feel about inviting your friends to join you in Sunday school?
a) very comfortable   b) moderately comfortable
c) slightly uncomfortable   d) not comfortable at all

15. Finish this sentence: The primary reason I attend my youth group's weeknight meetings is . . . (circle one)
a) to see my friends   b) my parents make me
c) to learn about God   d) to play fun group games
e) my youth leader asks me to go   f) to get advice for life
g) other (please list here)

16. What's the best part of the programming in your youth group's weeknight meetings?
a) the group games   b) the singing   c) the teaching time
d) the skits/dramas   e) the prayer time   f) the group discussions
g) other (please list here)

17. Which is the best night for a weeknight meeting?
a) Monday   b) Tuesday   c) Wednesday   d) Thursday   e) Friday

18. How important to you are small groups in a youth group?
a) very important   b) moderately important
c) slightly important   d) not important at all

19. Finish this sentence: The main purpose of a small group should be . . . (circle one)
a) to pray for the members of the small group
b) to deepen relationships with other Christians
c) to study the Bible more in-depth
d) to evangelize or help others become Christians
e) to create a support group for the members of the small group
f) to challenge the members of the small group to grow spiritually
g) other (please list here)

20. Finish this sentence: In regard to small groups, I would like to . . .
a) become more involved in a small group
b) continue my current level of involvement in a small group
c) become less involved in a small group
d) this question doesn't apply to me; I'm not interested in small groups at all

21. Have you ever made a life-changing decision at a camp or retreat that continues to have a positive impact on your relationship with God today?
a) yes   b) no

22. Finish this sentence: The things I like best about a camp or retreat are . . . (circle up to two)
a) getting time away from home   b) building deeper friendships
c) more concentrated learning about God   d) pulling practical jokes
e) hearing new speakers   f) meeting new people
g) trying new activities   h) campfire meetings
i) camp food   j) outdoor activities
k) nighttime games/activities   l) other (please list here)

23. What's the maximum amount you'd pay for a one-week camping experience with your youth group?
a) under $100   b) between $100-$200   c) between $200-$300
d) between $300-$400   e) between $400-$500   f) more than $500

24. Where would you most like for you and your youth group to participate in a service/mission project?
a) right in your community
b) somewhere within your state
c) somewhere outside your state, but in the U.S.
d) somewhere outside the U.S.

25. How often do you think you and your youth group should participate in a service/mission project?
a) at least once a month
b) once or twice a year
c) once every two years
d) once every three years
e) once every four years
f) never

26. What's the most important consideration for you when deciding whether or not to participate in a service/mission project? (circle one)
a) which of my friends are going
b) the type of work we'll do
c) the cost
d) the accommodations
e) safety issues
f) the location
g) the Bible's encouragement to serve
h) whether or not fun activities are included along with the work
i) other (please list here)

27. Which types of special events do you like to see in your youth group? (circle up to two)
a) Christian music concerts
b) spectator sporting events
c) movie nights
d) youth rallies
e) pizza nights
f) lock-ins
g) swim parties
h) hayrides
i) amusement parks
j) skate parties
k) game nights
l) picnics
m) hiking/outdoor activities
n) snow skiing
o) water skiing
p) beach parties
q) other (please list here)

28. How much can you typically afford to pay for a special event with your youth group?
a) less than $1.00
b) less than $5.00
c) less than $10.00
d) less than $20.00
e) less than $30.00
f) less than $50.00
g) other (please list here)

29. Finish this sentence: My youth group's special events . . . (circle one)
a) are very helpful for reaching out to my non-Christian friends
b) are somewhat helpful for reaching out to my non-Christian friends
c) are little help for reaching out to my non-Christian friends
d) are no help at all in reaching out to my non-Christian friends

30. What's the reason behind your answer to the previous question?

31. As a whole, how much influence do volunteer leaders have on your level of involvement in your youth group?
a) not much   b) a little   c) a moderate amount   d) a great deal

32. What qualities do you want your youth pastor to look for most when he or she is selecting a volunteer youth leader? (circle up to two)
a) commitment to Jesus b) caring attitude c) good listener
d) good teacher   e) loyalty   f) encouraging personality
g) honesty   h) wisdom   i) well-informed of teen trends
j) fun-loving   k) not too young l) not too old
m) other (please list here)

33. Which statement best describes how you'd feel about your parents being volunteer leaders in your youth group?
a) I'm strongly against the idea   b) I'm moderately against the idea
c) makes no difference to me   d) I'm moderately for the idea
e) I'm strongly for the idea

34. If you could choose the next topic your youth group studied, what would it be?

35. What topic are you sick of studying in youth group?

36. May we contact you later for a 15-minute follow-up phone interview?
a) Yes   b) No
If yes, please print your name and phone number (with area code) below:

Appendix 2: About Reach Workcamps

Reach Workcamps is a nonprofit Christian organization offering quality, week-long workcamp experiences that enable teenagers to be actively involved in home repair projects for our nation's needy and elderly. The projects selected are supervised by professionals, appropriate for the age group attending a camp, and include things such as weatherization, roofing repair, construction of wheelchair ramps and porches, and more. All repairs are made at no cost to the home's residents.

Daily devotions and faith-building evening programs during each workcamp encourage spiritual growth and maturity in teens' relationships with one another and with Jesus Christ. In addition, Reach supports Christian churches and organizations and actively encourages workcamp participants to adopt a lifestyle of serving those in need in their home communities.

"Through reaching out to others," says founder Mike Jones, "Reach equips teen Christians with the skills and opportunities necessary to impact their world for Jesus Christ."

For a free subscription to the *Reach WC Network* newsletter or for information about a workcamp near you, contact Reach Workcamps at:

> P.O. Box 1614
> Loveland, CO 80539
> (888) 732-2492
> www.reachwc.org

ABOUT THE AUTHOR

Mike Nappa is the president and founder of Nappaland Communications Inc., a media organization located in Colorado. He has served in both professional and volunteer youth ministry for sixteen years and is the author or co-author of many books related to youth ministry and family, including *Faith Happens!* (Standard Publishing), *It's a Sheep's Life* (Standard), *Get Real: Making Core Christian Beliefs Relevant to Teenagers* (Group Publishing) and *Bore No More!* (Group).

Mike has also contributed to many popular magazines, including *Living with Teenagers, Group, Junior High Ministry, Campus Life, Breakaway, Brio, Christian Single* and *ParentLife*.

To contact Mike, send email to: Nappaland@aol.com.